T0028601

Veneration Rites of
CURANDERISMO
❧ ✳ ❧

"Once again Erika Buenaflor brings us a useful, powerful, and game-changing modern look at ancient wisdom. This book not only helps us cultivate a walkable bridge between ourselves and our ancestors, it provides much-needed rituals around the important transitions of death, dying, and grief. Every practitioner interested in ancestral work, regardless of their cultural background, needs a copy of this book."

J. ALLEN CROSS, AUTHOR OF *AMERICAN BRUJERIA: MODERN MEXICAN AMERICAN FOLK MAGIC*

"The wisdom of the ancestors vibrates from the pages of Erika's book and infuses the reader with warmth, comfort, and the feeling of coming home to ourselves. Brimming with fascinating history, heartfelt stories, and accessible exercises, Erika seamlessly weaves a pathway for us to reconnect and reclaim the strength and power of those who came before. Erika is a knowledgeable and trusted *maestra* and offers us a tender and steady hand to help lead us to the full and joyous lives we are meant to live. This book is a rare gift, Erika is a gift, and we are all better for it."

ROBYN MORENO, CURANDERISMO PRACTITIONER AND AUTHOR OF *GET ROOTED: RECLAIM YOUR SOUL, SERENITY, AND SISTERHOOD THROUGH THE HEALING MEDICINE OF THE GRANDMOTHERS*

"Ancestral veneration rites are an ancient form of healing, blessing, spiritual interaction, and renewal. Erika not only offers spiritual guidance and wisdom but also shows ancient techniques and methods for the revival of these rites. Erika's experiences, deep knowledge, and love for our ancestors and future generations to come shines through every page."

LAURA DAVILA, AUTHOR OF *MEXICAN SORCERY:*
A PRACTICAL GUIDE TO BRUJERIA DE RANCHO

"This book nourished my spirit like a healing broth of bones and herbs. I immediately felt the urge to strengthen my own practice with the rites and rituals brought to life within its pages."

FELICIA COCOTZIN RUIZ, AUTHOR OF *EARTH MEDICINES:*
ANCESTRAL WISDOM, HEALING RECIPES,
AND WELLNESS RITUALS FROM A CURANDERA

Veneration Rites of
CURANDERISMO

INVOKING THE SACRED ENERGY
OF OUR ANCESTORS

ERIKA BUENAFLOR, M.A., J.D.

Bear & Company
Rochester, Vermont

Bear & Company
One Park Street
Rochester, Vermont 05767
www.BearandCompanyBooks.com

Text stock is SFI certified

Bear & Company is a division of Inner Traditions International

Copyright © 2023 by Erika Buenaflor

All rights reserved. No part of this book may be reproduced or utilized in any form
or by any means, electronic or mechanical, including photocopying, recording, or by
any information storage and retrieval system, without permission in writing from the
publisher.

*Note to the reader: This book is intended as an informational guide. The remedies,
approaches, and techniques described herein are meant to supplement, and not to be a
substitute for, professional medical care or treatment. They should not be used to treat
a serious ailment without prior consultation with a qualified health care professional.*

Cataloging-in-Publication Data for this title is available from the Library of Congress

ISBN 978-1-59143-496-2 (print)
ISBN 978-1-59143-497-9 (ebook)

Printed and bound in the United States by Lake Book Manufacturing, LLC
The text stock is SFI certified. The Sustainable Forestry Initiative® program
promotes sustainable forest management.

10   9   8   7   6   5   4   3   2   1

Text design and layout by Virginia Scott Bowman
This book was typeset in Garamond Premier Pro and Gill Sans with Frutiger and
Latienne used as the display typeface
Photos courtesy of Ancient Americas at LACMA may be found at AncientAmericas.org.

To send correspondence to the author of this book, mail a first-class letter to the
author c/o Inner Traditions • Bear & Company, One Park Street, Rochester, VT
05767, and we will forward the communication, or contact the author directly at
RealizeYourBliss.com.

Contents

FOREWORD

The Great Weaving

Let me tell you about an ancestor of mine: my mother María Estela Rodríguez, who passed in 2008.

When I was a child, my mother made a point to remind me, one of four children she had with my father, that we had roots with the Tarahumara people of Chihuahua, Mexico, where my mother was born and raised. Almost anyone with long ties in Chihuahua has Tarahumara ancestry. They are considered the second-largest Indigenous North American people north of Mexico City after the Diné (Navajo).

Now most Mexican migrants to the United States—and I lived in barrios with generations of Mexicans almost all my life—can't tell you what Indigenous connections they may have. This, of course, is due to generations of "de-Indianization." Now to be clear, what's considered "Mexican" is a great mix of cultures, including all "races" and ethnicities. There's also an immense degree of "Hispanicization" due to three hundred years of Spanish colonial rule until Mexico became its own nation in 1821. After that the process of "Mexicanization" began, what any nation-state must do to secure a "home market"—establish a cultural identity tied to common land, language, and laws.

Nonetheless, our deepest root is Indigenous North American. On top of this, there are around twenty-five million people in Mexico (more than any country in the western hemisphere) who are tribal and often speak original languages. In fact, Mexico today has sixty-eight official languages drawing from up to three hundred language groups and variants. One of these groups are the Tarahumara, who also call themselves Rarámuri.

Once aware, you can see the Indigenous in many Mexican faces, in their inflections, and in their customs. Many words in Mexico are of Nahuatl origin, some of which have entered the English language like avocado, chocolate, taco, coyote, ocelot, and tomato. In Spanish, Nahuatl words included common ones. My father often used "escuincle" to mean a child, although originally it was the Nahuatl word for dog.

Of my siblings, I was the only one enraptured when my mother related about the Tarahumara/Rarámuri. Later, as an adult, I visited the Sierra Tarahumara in Chihuahua, home to the famous Copper Canyon, where Tarahumaras still live with their relatively intact traditional ways, speaking their original tongues, with tens of thousands living in caves, some of the last cave dwellers in the world.

I also recall my mother having an altar in the living rooms of our many houses with candles, religious icons (La Guadalupe, Jesus Christ, and saints), but also photos of ancestors like my grandmother and grandfather on my mother's side, both whom I never knew, and even a great-grandmother, Manuela, with the face and stature of a Tarahumara woman.

Once, at age thirteen, I had painful fungus growths on my feet when I worked in a car wash with my brother cleaning up the place. We used hoses and lots of water that nightly soaked through my sneakers. We rarely went to a doctor in those days, but my mother took me to one, who didn't know what to do about these growths. He gave me ointments, none of which worked. My mother then brought in her brother, my Tío Kiko (who was also my *nino*—godfather). They turned to ways that had to be kept underground. I'm sure my father forbade my mother to use the *curandera* traditions of the homeland in the United States, but they must have felt they had no choice.

Tío Kiko put marijuana leaves (when marijuana was illegal to possess and was not yet known in popular culture as having medicinal properties) into a gourd. He filled the gourd with "añejo" (aged) tequila, then left the gourd hanging off a clothesline all night long. The next day, with prayers in Spanish and I believe in Rarámuri, he cut the growths on my foot (a bloody mess), then placed the leaves over the cuts, changing them periodically. In a matter of days, the growths were gone. When I went to the clinic for a follow-up appointment, the doctor expressed great surprise. However, we kept the cure a secret.

In this book you now hold in your hands, Erika Buenaflor reminds us that these remnants of ancient wisdom practices are not unusual and are in fact endemic to our Mexicanness (as well as among those from El Salvador, Guatemala, Nicaragua, Honduras, and other Central American countries—areas known generally as Mesoamerica). We still carry indigeneity in our DNA as "genetic memory," whether we are conscious of it or not. Despite conquest, forced colonial-bred identities, and other traumas of these countries—as well as the racist and classist discriminations prevalent in the United States—we are Indigenous to this land at the deepest layers of our being.

Like Erika, I chose to bring ancestral knowledge to my life, my family, and my community, now for some thirty years. This includes the renowned cultural center and bookstore cofounded by my wife Trini and myself over twenty years ago in Los Angeles: Tia Chucha's Centro Cultural & Bookstore, which was established on an Indigenous-based philosophy, and has teachings of Nahuatl, Mexicayotl cosmology, *curanderismo,* as well as "Temachtia Quetzacoat," our resident Mexica (Aztec) Kalpulli and Danza circle. I've also done ceremony and spiritual practices among the Lakota, O'odham, Diné, Paiute-Shoshone, Tataviam (San Fernando Valley), Pipil (El Salvador), Maya (Mexico and Guatemala), and Quechua (Peru). In 1998, Diné elders in Lukachukai, Arizona of the Navajo Nation spiritually adopted my wife Trini, and consequently the whole family.

Trini and I (and my eldest grandson Ricardo) also received Mexica names based in the *tonalpohualli* calendar in 2019 guided by elders of the Kalpulli Tlaque Nahuaque. My eldest son, Ramiro (Ricardo's dad) is a Mexica Danzante (Aztec dancer). And we're part of the Native

American Turtle Lodge in Sylmar, California, where Trini also facilitates the Hummingbird Women's Lodge, now for over ten years.

While this ancestral knowledge is always there—accessible in nature, our own natures, the nature of relationships, and the nature of the divine—there is no purity of traditions anymore. Christianity and other Western ideas and practices are intertwined with venerable ways. In my decades of ceremony on the rez, and in countries such as Mexico, even among the Rarámuri, the colonialization holds are still there, although transfigured. Nonetheless, veneration of our ancestors—that is respectful and meaningful relationships with the past (the abuelx)— is alive and well. We honor all the threads. Our ties are persistent, not just occasional.

Erika's well-wrought teachings, rituals, and instructions, much of which were taught to her by elders and curanderx, but also from extensive study, are antidotes to the various physical, mental, emotional, cultural, and spiritual ailments we've endured for over five hundred years. The ground she covers is quite enormous. Some of the sources she names have been challenged, questioned by elders and others. But knowing all of this is not bad if one can also rely on the instinct to know what is authentic, what rings true, and what is lasting beyond history, beyond politics, beyond human naming and renaming. I'm convinced Erika has this instinct, something in her bones, not just in her head.

What we do know is that a mythic imagination means both healing and ceremony exist for any of the troubles that appear so singular and unfathomable in our day. If one understands the process, there is always the possibility of regeneration—renewal from decay, rebirth from death. And going to the ancestors, to our deepest sources, is key to the depth of alignment and healing we can finally realize. An Indigenous elder once told me that calling on the ancestors is like appealing to a "Legislature of the Dead"—not just any dead, but the ones chosen or elected by prayers, intentions, and by who best represent the values you exude as their progeny. These are the real "living dead," the abuelx who still reside inside us.

That's the Indigenous way, the Tarahumara way, the way of all original peoples of these vast lands. Erika is reminding us to remember. If we are in crisis, it's because the barriers, literal and figurative prisons, as well as colonial mindsets and psychologies, must die so the powerful ancestral-guided rituals and practices, even if reimagined, can burst forth as a great weaving of the past, present, and future.

And for this I give a hearty *tlazohkamati*—thank you!

LUIS J. RODRÍGUEZ (MIXCÓATL ITZTLACUILOH),
SAN FERNANDO, CALIFORNIA

LUIS J. RODRÍGUEZ (Mixcóatl Itztlacuiloh) is the author of sixteen multigenre books, including the memoirs *Always Running, La Vida Loca, Gang Days in L.A.,* and *It Calls You Back: An Odyssey Through Love, Addiction, Revolutions and Healing,* both from Atria Books/Simon & Schuster. He's also author of *Hearts & Hands: Creating Community in Violent Times* and *From Our Land to Our Land: Essays, Journeys & Imaginings from a Native Xicanx Writer,* both from Seven Stories Press.

Ancient Mesoamerican and Curanderismo Ancestral Veneration

NEPANTLA SPIRITUALITY

In Nepantla spirituality, those who have been historically marginalized, their cultures and spiritual practices demonized, derided, and misappropriated by others, reclaim this liminal middle space, humble, empowered, and ready to define their path, their purpose, and their spirituality for themselves.

Nepantla is a space of liminality, constant change, realizing, and becoming, where truly changing, realizing, and becoming are norms.

In Nepantla spirituality, we unshackle ourselves from the status quo's definitions of who we are and the boxes they put us in and reclaim ourselves for ourselves. Reclaim what this liminal space—Nepantla—is for us. What spirituality means for us.

In Nepantla spirituality, we are rooted by our ancestors. Our ancestors are the ones who anchor us with a feeling of belonging to something greater than us, something divine and beautiful. They guide us as we shape, reclaim, and define our path and purpose. They root us into a history that becomes a part of our beloved identities.

In Nepantla spirituality, we are the healers, healing our ancestral lineage, being healed by our ancestors, reclaiming our esteemed ancestors.

Welcome to Nepantla Spirituality.

Erika Buenaflor

❖ ❖ ❖

Ancestral veneration rites, practices, and beliefs have vibrant and deep-rooted traditions in ancient Mesoamerica, approximately 1200 BCE to 1521 CE. Ancestors were treated as active agents who played direct roles among their heirs, communities, and polities, often decades after their physical deaths. Ancestors were honored and invoked for many reasons, including to: provide guidance, protection, and aid in divergent cultural, religious, and political situations; legitimize different power dynamics; sanctify access and rights to resources; maintain social cohesion within descent groups; and facilitate the creation and re-creation of social memory and identity.[1] They were seen and treated as a powerful force not to be trifled with. Archaeological finds demonstrate extensive and ongoing ancestral veneration rituals performed at funerary pyramids, burials, graves, tombs, and interments* among both non-elite and elite sectors of society, and in both domestic and public ritual contexts.

Abundant iconographic evidence and pictorial imagery also show the importance of ancestors, their direct and ongoing agency, and the pivotal roles they played.[3] The Indigenous peoples who eventually aligned themselves with the conquistadores for various complex reasons, including to overthrow the Mexica, apprised Hernán Cortés, a sixteenth-century Spanish conquistador, that ancestors provided guidance and counsel. Cortés leveraged this in his first conversation with Moctezuma II, the second-to-last ruler of the Aztec empire. Without Moctezuma II stating anything about them, Cortés acknowledged that his ancestors had already told him that the Spaniards were not natives of this land but came from another, distant location.[4] Cortés understood the importance of the Mesoamerican traditions of obtaining ancestral counsel and guidance and attempted to legitimize their presence in the Americas by drawing upon this knowledge.

---

*A simple interment is an unlined hole or pit in the bedrock surface or structural fill, or a grave in which the living placed a body directly into the fill during construction. Interments that are described as "in vessel" were placed inside a ceramic bowl or jar.[2]

Ancestors were believed to be comprised of sacred essence energy or soul energy that could be continued, reborn, or renewed into or become a part of the bodies of their heirs, animals, insects, *milpas* (corn fields), orchards, sacred physical spaces and tools, as well as the cycles of solar and cosmic re-creation and death.[5] The soul energy of ancestors was also often believed and treated as the same sacred "stuff" that circulated throughout the cosmos, the means by which innate life force increased and gave power to make organisms come into being, live, grow, and reproduce.[6] Ancestors were also believed to be traversing into the physical realms on particular days, during certain rites, at sacred spaces, into sacred objects, and through people, animals, or insects.

In this book, I will highlight the diverse and dynamic ancestral veneration rites of the ancient Mesoamerican peoples and how we can draw from these traditions to not only enliven and inspire our ancestral veneration practices, but to take us deeper in our personal healing journeys of awareness, decolonization,* and personal and ancestral reclamation. Whatever our background is, we have all been adversely affected, in one way or another, by the hundreds of years of worldwide colonization.

---

*It is important to first define colonization generally before I identify what decolonization is in the context of this book, particularly because it inherently involves a dismantling of colonization and its different facets. Colonization is typically identified as external and internal colonization, wherein both are very interdependent in order to maintain their success and proliferation. External colonization is often identified as the exploitation of land, in which the focus is on extracting goods like cacao, silk, or sugar, or resources like human labor, foods, minerals, or oil, in order to increase the wealth and power of the colonizers. Internal colonization is typically identified as the control or exploitation of the people through their hearts and minds, using cultural, political, and economic institutions. The faces of the colonizer have changed throughout the histories of colonization. But their violent programs—aims and operations—are essentially the same: exploitation of the land and its people. Whether we are BIPOC or White we have all been affected by colonization. I am addressing cultural decolonization, especially as it relates to spirituality.

In this context, decolonization is typically rooted with an individual being willing and able to reclaim sovereignty and agency over their identities. We reclaim and stand in our power to define and reclaim our identities, which encompass our ancestral connections, and what faith and spirituality is to us.

The more we strengthen our connection with our ancestors, the more they can then guide, aid, and intervene in our lives more directly and seamlessly, as well as infuse us with their soul energy. With stronger soul energy we have more energy to finish our more mundane tasks, facilitate healing and spiritual work for ourselves and others, and manifest with greater impeccability. Whether we can create a long and detailed genetic family tree of our ancestors or we don't have any knowledge of our grandparents (or even our parents), this book offers diverse ways of connecting with our ancestors from many different spectrums.

Ancestral veneration practices, at their most fundamental level, can help us feel rooted, offer a comforting sense of belonging, and provide exciting opportunities to stand in our power and shape, create, and re-create our identities. The soul energies of our ancestors can give us the necessary energy and strength to pursue and be consistent in our journeys of healing, understanding, and self-awareness, and give vigor to our manifestation endeavors. By working with and honoring our ancestors, we can be blessed with their soul energy, guidance, gifts, talents, and healing.

Working with our ancestors also provides beautiful opportunities for deep healing for ourselves, our families, and all of our relations. The traumas that our ancestors experienced, as well as their possible wrongdoings, are often played out or experienced by us as opportunities to be resolved and healed. When we offer this healing to our ancestors, we also receive this healing and so does our family. Strengthening our connections to our ancestors also provides opportunities for us to re-envision who or what we choose to be associated with, how we perceive our roots, and our own related identities in positive and empowering ways.

Additionally, working with our ancestors often entails working with our shadow aspects, breaking ancestral curses, healing our fragmented identities, and, well, it is not always pretty and light. It can be messy, confusing, and full of idiosyncrasies. But it is definitely worth it to find the strength to reclaim ourselves, our identities, our roots, and our ancestors, and to consciously choose our ancestors and who we want as part of our spiritual entourage. Once upon a time I felt completely disassociated from my ancestral roots, and now any *limpia* rites or *brujería* I practice on my ancestral altar is unstoppable.

Inspired by my ancient Mesoamerican ancestors and my curanderx* mentors, I treat ancestors as entities comprised of soul energy, power, wisdom, healing, and knowledge, which can be accessed by practices of veneration. I draw from the ancient Mesoamericans' understanding of the soul as having different expressions of animating energies that were concentrated in different regions of the body.

The Mexica, for example, believed there were three prominent soul-animating energies:

1. *teyolía,* concentrated in the heart and was constant in some-one's life
2. *ihiyotl,* concentrated in the liver or stomach and was also con-stant in someone's life
3. *tonalli,* concentrated in the head, hair, blood, and nails, and could leave the body during life, primarily due to different kinds of traumas[7]

Many of the ancestral veneration rites at the time of death and thereafter often involved helping the ancestor regain any soul pieces that may have been lost during their lives and strengthen their soul energies in the afterlife. Depending on the strength or wholeness of the ancestors' soul energies, their ancestors could reside and traverse differ-ent living and nonordinary realms, could intervene on behalf of their heirs with greater expediency, and could experience rebirth, continua-tion, cosmic cycles, and renewal in dynamic and divergent ways, includ-ing infusing their heirs with stronger soul energies, possibly even deified soul energies.

Today, curanderx are the practitioners of curanderismo, a Latin

---

*I continue to follow the trend of progressive Latinx communities that are using the *x* suffix in place of *-a/-o* and *-as/-os* at the end of gendered words. The use of the *x* is intended to transcend static gender binaries.

American shamanic healing practice. This eclectic practice can incorporate Judeo-Christian (especially Catholic), Native American, Caribbean, Spanish, Moorish, and African practices and beliefs. Its roots, however, lie in the beliefs, practices, and methodologies of the Indigenous peoples of the Americas. I did most of my training as a curandera in the Yucatán with two curanderx who had lived all of their lives in the Yucatán, and with two others who were trained in Yucatec Maya practices and were also versed in Mexica or Nahua* shamanic traditions. My more than two decades of training and experience as a curandera have been heavily influenced by Mesoamerican Indigenous traditions, especially in the understanding of ancestors and ancestral veneration rites.

For the purposes of this book, an ancestor is anyone who has ever been incarnated here on Earth or elsewhere who we want to honor as our ancestor. Per ancient Mesoamerican traditions, just because a family member passed did not necessarily mean they would be revered as an ancestor, even if that family member was loved and remembered. And ancestors do not need to be people related to us by blood. Just as deep love, resentment, and other unresolved matters can keep blood family members connected to one another in subsequent lives, so do strong affinities to something, such as a vocation, culture, or a connection to sacred land. In this context, affinities are made up of strong passion energies that continue to link similar energies together throughout many lives and realities.

This is critical as many people are unaware of their blood lineage or do not have an affinity to a deceased family member in their

---

*The terms *Mexica* and *Nahua* have often been used interchangeably to talk about the same group of people within the Aztec empire. The term *Nahua* has also been used to denote the Indigenous peoples of Central Mexico, mainly because the Spanish friars incorporated and used Nahuatl as a lingua franca among the Indigenous peoples of the Mesoamerican plateau. Recently, the term *Nahua* is often used to describe the many Indigenous peoples of Mexico and El Salvador. The term *Mexica* is generally understood as an ethnic marker that designates the Nahuatl-speaking group that inhabited Tenochtitlan and Tlatelolco, the two island settlements that comprised Mexico and later became the center of Mexico City.

blood lineage. Nonetheless, they feel an inexplicable soul connection to a cultural legend, deceased mentor, or sacred land. But they are not necessarily from that culture, are unrelated to the deceased mentor, or are not from the area to which they feel a strong connection. This connection is nonetheless deeply intuitive—a relentless yet calm voice-feeling-sensation-knowingness of an inexplicable soul connection. The connection is likely an ancestral one.

Ancestral veneration rites often went hand in hand with the creation and re-creation of social identities in ancient Mesoamerica and the divergent expressions of revered ancestors as soul energy. Although the veneration of blood ancestors was likely the norm, there were numerous instances where an ancestral connection was claimed, reenvisioned, and re-created, even when the people likely did not have a blood relation to the ancestors they claimed as ancestors.

The most notable and well-known example of this is the Mexica's claimed ancestral connection to the illustrious Toltecs of the early Postclassic period (900–1000 CE), and Teotihuacán of the Classic period (100–700 CE). The Mexica were foreigners to the basin of Mexico, the lands of the Toltec and Teotihuacán. Yet, after the Mexica became more powerful, they claimed an ancestral connection to these magnificent polities.[8]

Burial and ancestral veneration rituals were critical and complex components of ongoing processes by which ancient Mesoamerican communities were continually redefining and renewing themselves. As Catherine Bell, ritual theoretician, asserts, ritual is like language not because it is a text whose symbolic meanings must be uncovered, but because rituals are actions that generate meanings in the specific context of other sets of meaningful actions and discourses. Ritual is established in the context in which it is enacted.[9]

In this book, I will explore ancient Mesoamerican ancestral ritual practices by comparing and contrasting various sources, including: funerary pyramids, graves, divergent interment and burial practices and locations and the sacred items found at these sites; mythologies concerning who was an ancestor, the dispensation of an ancestor, the management of an ancestor's soul, and the rebirth of an ancestor's soul energy; illustrative, sculptural, and architectural authorities; and the pre- and post-contact codices; and sixteenth-, seventeenth-, and eighteenth-century ethnohistorical records. I will delve into the observable aspects of burials, skeletal remains, and the art and objects found at these sites to assess how communities and families valued individuals and the unique and diverse patterns of their mortuary practices. In some instances, I will also include the teachings of my curanderx mentors regarding relevant rites and practices to provide suggestive analogies, rather than definitive conclusions as to the meaning of these rituals.

Although we are delving into ancient Mesoamerican rituals and practices that we can no longer witness, we can find tendrils of that meaning in other related lines of archaeological, iconographic, and epigraphic data.[10] The understanding of what constituted Mesoamerican ancestral veneration practices will include an analysis of the complexity of their ties and, through them, their likenesses and differences explained—when applicable and this information is available.[11] As Mesoamerican scholar Alfredo López Austin asserts, "A common history and local histories interacted dialectically to form a Mesoamerican vision in which the variants acquired extraordinary individual peculiarities."[12]

Ancient Mesoamerican ancestral veneration rituals involved complex and multilayered performances and practices, each of whose individual criteria (grave type, orientation, position, furniture, burial items) can be seen as parts of individual and multidimensional interwoven networks of references.[13] The location of graves, design, art, rituals, and sacred items placed at burial sites were critical in facilitating and enticing their ancestors' intervention, aid, and visitation, as well as the rebirth and renewal of the ancestors' soul energy and, in some cases, their deification. While the living, of course, negotiated and appropriated their own unique understandings of these rites, they performed scripts that contained a common core of ancient Mesoamerican beliefs concerning ancestral veneration. This book will delve into these common core beliefs, as well as their nuanced divergent literal and performed expressions.

This book will also survey the unique regional and temporal ancestral veneration rites of the more influential city-states and cultures of the Classic (250–909 CE) and Postclassic (909–1697 CE) Central Mexican and Maya peoples. These influential city-states and cultures will include: Teotihuacán, the Zapotec, the Maya lowland city-states encompassing the northern part of Central America, in the Yucatán peninsula of Mexico, Guatemala, and Belize; the Toltec; the Mixtec; and the Aztec empire.* Because so many ancestral veneration rites, beliefs, and mythologies were influenced in some way by Teotihuacán, the threads of examination often begin with this state-level society.[14]

Teotihuacán's local population buried their dead according to local canon, and while foreigners typically interred according to their specific cultural traditions, they also adopted some Teotihuacán practices.[16] Teotihuacán's influence of ancestral veneration also reached into many Maya lowland city-states, such as Copan in Honduras, and the reach of other influential city-states was also often absorbed by Teotihuacán.[17] Remnants of Teotihuacán's ancestral veneration practices and mythologies was also expressed in their own unique ways by the Postclassic Mixtec, Toltec, and peoples of the Aztec empire.

It is also important to point out that the examination of their ancestral veneration rites, especially as it relates to burial practices at diverse sites, is still ongoing, and there are inherent issues with this continuing work. Most of the research has been performed at the magnificent sites with easier-to-detect temples and within plazas of the cities where elite ancestral rites and practices reigned. The focus

---

*In this context, I use the term *Aztec empire* to describe the various city-states that the Mexica had conquered of the Anahuac plateau—extending from the coast of the Gulf of Mexico to the Pacific Ocean and as far south as Chiapas and Guatemala—as well as their triple alliance with Texcoco and Tlacopan, an alliance that was more honorary than actual by the beginning of the sixteenth century. The Aztec empire consisted of: 200,000 to 250,000 people who lived in Tenochtitlan; approximately over one million people who lived in the Valley of Mexico; and another two to three million who dwelt in the surrounding valleys of Central Mexico, when Cortés and his army arrived in 1519.[15]

to uncover and understand the ancestral veneration rites of the non-elite classes has however received a greater emphasis in the last few decades. But there is still much to learn about the nuances of the beautiful ancestral veneration rites of the non-elite classes.[18] Also, many burial sites have been severely looted, and the sacred items that could have provided greater insight into these traditions are no longer publicly available or were reconstituted or melted into something else, especially precious metals. Conquistadors Hernán Cortés and Bernal Díaz del Castilloboth documented the immense looting of Cu de Huchilobos.[19] Regardless, a significant amount of work has been done to provide a rich and colorful understanding of Mesoamerican ancestral veneration practices.

BREAKDOWN OF THIS BOOK

In every chapter, I interweave my personal or my clients' experiences in connecting with, healing, and reclaiming our ancestors to ground the ancient and contemporary ancestral veneration rites with tangible and often raw and vulnerable stories and sites of decolonization. The first chapter explores the diverse burial practices of the ancient Mesoamerican peoples and assess who took on the prestigious role of being identified as an ancestor. Not all deceased individuals became ancestors; rather, the role of ancestor was reserved for leaders and prominent lineage members. Their various kinds of burial rites, and whether a burial rite was performed at all, revealed whether a deceased individual would take an esteemed role of ancestor and for how long. We will then delve into considerations and curanderismo ceremonies for choosing our ancestor(s) and what roles they may take.

The second chapter examines the different *ofrendas* (offerings) they left at the funerary sites of their ancestors, which were multivalent in purpose and meaning and typically and most importantly facilitated a stronger bond between the living and their ancestors. These offerings enticed their ancestors' intervention, aid, and visitation, as well as ensured their comfort and well-being. They also procured continuing and active lines of communication and relationships between the living and their ancestors and enabled them to cross into each other's worlds. We will use this wisdom to explore our ancestral altar-making practices, sacred tools for these altars, their locations, and rituals to continue to develop our relationships with our ancestors.

The third chapter focuses on the numerous ceremonies the ancient Mesoamerican peoples engaged in to honor their ancestors. There were some rites that continued until the ancestor was believed to have reached an afterlife destination; others were associated with their solar and ritual calendars. We then explore our own sacred ceremonies and performances to honor and love our ancestors and strengthen our connections with them, as well as strengthen our connections with our ancestors as a family with ritual craft-making. These activities can often inspire our family and children and be incredibly healing for our inner child to feel a sense of pride toward their familial and cultural connections.

The fourth chapter looks at their diverse comprehension of the rebirth, renewal, and continuation of an ancestor's soul energy and the many ways they could manifest. Their soul energy, for example, could become world trees and plants of economic and symbolic import, be inherited by their heirs, participate in different kinds of cosmic cycles, flow in the sea or ocean waiting for their rebirth, experience a solar apotheosis, become a part of universal soul energy, become spirits or gods, or become a part of a mythological or actual animal.[20] Using this sacred wisdom, we delve into rites that invite the souls of our ancestors to share space with and be reborn in our gardens and take a more active role in intervening on our behalf, as well as rituals to invoke and strengthen our connection with them.

The fifth chapter delves into the deification of esteemed ancestors and how this often enabled special powers within the ancestor's lineage, including journeying, getting insight, and accessing medicine, messages, and wisdom from nonordinary realms, as well as bolstering their magic, shapeshifting skills, vocation, and, of course, legitimizing their power and rule. Mythologies depicted ancestors as deities or as deified energy. This deified ancestral energy was then transferred into a ruler at birth and during accession rituals. It can be an incredibly humbling and positively transformative experience when we can accept that those we identify as our ancestors are divine energy and that we are also comprised of divine energy. We then open to sweet healing ceremonies to reclaim our ancestors and ourselves as pure divine sacred energy to invite more wisdom and healing for ourselves and our familial and ancestral lineages, as well as authentic practices of self-love and limpia rites to empower our ancestral veneration and healing practices.

The epilogue weaves in the ancestral rites highlighted in this book to purge the grief of the death of loved ones in safe ritualized spaces and facilitate their graceful transition. One of the things that was a little bit surprising was the increasing number of clients who came to me for these exact two reasons, almost immediately after I began doing the research for this book. It was almost as if all of our ancestors conspired together to ensure that there would be greater access for people to have healthier ways of processing the loss of a loved one or a loved one who was about to transition. Despite the gratitude of my clients as to how these rites have helped them, for whatever reason, I debated inserting this in the book. But I knew I received another strong nudge to share how these ancestral rites can help us during one of the most difficult times of our lives, the death of a loved one, when my editor asked me for a conclusion for this book.

AIMS OF THIS BOOK

One of the principal goals of this book is to decolonize and reclaim sacred ancient Mesoamerican practices and traditions in ways that can inform, inspire, and heal our cultural and ancestral ties and identities. This reclamation is, of course, not limited to Latinx and Xicanx communities, and it is definitely for us. Due to complex histories of colonization and war, many of us often have threads of family ties that have been both the colonizer and the colonized. In the case of ancient

Mesoamerican Indigenous peoples, our sacred practices and traditions have been ridiculed, derided, and misappropriated for hundreds of years. Today these practices still go without the recognition or genuine understanding they deserve.

The reclamation of ancestors and the willingness to heal our ancestral lineages lends itself to a Nepantla spirituality. Nepantla spirituality integrates the understanding that, while Nepantla is a liminal middle space, it is also a space where we recognize the malleability of identities and claim our power to define who we choose as our ancestors, what we will root ourselves to, and how we envision them and us. It blends nonreligious, pagan, religious, and heart-centered practices—basically any kind of tradition or practice that involves believing in some kind of divine power and the relevant rites that arise.

Diego Durán, sixteenth-century missionary and ethnographer, first recorded the use of Nepantla when he questioned and reprimanded an Indigenous man about how he worked so hard for his money but then spent everything on a wedding that he invited the entire town to. The Indigenous man explained that they were still in Nepantla, in a middle space, and "they neither answered to one faith or the other or, better said, that they believed in God and at the same time keep their ancient customs and . . . rites."[21] Gloria Anzaldúa, Xicana theoretician and artist, refers to Nepantla as a dark cave of creativity that can foster a new state of understanding.[22] Lara Medina, Xicana theoretician, asserts, "Nepantla is the liminal space that can confuse its occupants but also has the ability to transform them."[23]

Ancestors in this ancient and contemporary vision of Nepantla are the ones who anchor us with a sense of belonging to something greater than us, divine and beautiful. They guide us as we shape, reclaim, and define our path and purpose in life. They root us into a history that becomes a part of our beloved identities.

We are no longer agonizing in a space of unsavory and uncertain ancestral lines, who may have been the colonized, the colonizer, the rapist, the raped, the dissociated—again unsavory. Rather, in this Nepantla spirituality, our chosen ancestors root us into an empowered space where we are the healers for those who came before us, and will come after us, and like our ancestors, are comprised of deified Xingonx, "badass" soul energy.

And in Nepantla spirituality, we show respect. Like our Mexica ancestors and many others who came before us, who claimed and appropriated the ancestors and cultures of their foreign relatives, the Toltecs and Teotihuacános, we learn their history, culture, and traditions, and give props where props need to be given. We the historically marginalized claim the power and right of decolonization, re-indigenization, and reappropriation, the agency to redefine ourselves for ourselves, our spirituality, our ancestors, our path, and our purpose.

The ancestral healing and veneration beliefs, practices, and traditions shared in this book can be used by anyone that can honor, respect, and give props to the Mesoamerican Indigenous peoples of these sacred practices, beliefs, and traditions. Appropriation is not a new thing and has been done repeatedly to the point wherein claiming clear authenticity and ownership of cultural traditions can easily lead to a slippery slope of dehistoricization and inaccuracies. Yet misappropriation, the taking of historically marginalized cultural traditions and practices without giving them any recognition, perpetuates the atrocities that have been committed against them.

Once again, a common thread that has been prevalent in all of my prior books, this reclamation is medicine in itself and can inspire us to weave our disassociated ancestral wisdom back into our heritage, as well as learn from, respect, and honor Indigenous traditions. I share my ancestors' traditions, practices, and beliefs with love and humility in my heart for anyone who is ready and willing to acknowledge these ancient ways and can be respectfully open to their beauty and sacrality. May the integration of these sacred traditions continue to heal us all and inspire us to reclaim our ancestors and root them into our beloved identities.

The second aim of this book is to not only enact the potential healing power of epistemology—claiming these sacred Indigenous traditions, practices, and histories as being worthy of being examined, further explored, and produced in our spiritual practices and ceremonies—but to make these sacred practices accessible and relevant for all of us. While I am incredibly grateful to many contemporary ancient Mesoamerican scholars, who are usually passionate and diligent, I also feel it is crucial to have these sacred histories, practices, and beliefs relevant and accessible to all audiences, including and especially mainstream audiences.

After the Spanish conquest, Mexico, along with many other Latin American countries, suffered over five hundred years of erased Indigenous genealogies to avoid various kinds of forced labor systems, and countless forms of systemic and cultural discrimination for having Indigenous blood, being Indigenous, looking Indigenous, or not looking Indigenous enough. The ancestral veneration practices identified in this book can be medicine for many of us, Latinx and others who, for whatever reason, are disconnected from their blood ancestors and elders, genealogical records are loaded with historical idiosyncrasies and possible erasures, as well as for those who have a strong bond or some kind of bond with their blood ancestors and elders. Although I was asked to remove the academic material or the bulk of it by most literary agents and publishers (except for Inner Traditions, of course), it is not enough to share anecdotal information about these ancient Mesoamerican ancestral veneration practices, especially if one of the aims is to decolonize and reclaim them. In these complex processes of decolonization, re-indigenization, and reclamation, it is often essential to critically place various sources, including the academic and spiritual in dialogue with one another.

In graduate school, I often found myself sobbing tears of joy and peace when reading codices, because I knew that my then-current intuitive rites were motivated in part by a subconscious remembrance of my ancestors. It is incredibly inspiring and healing to root our identities and spiritual practices in knowing why we have done what we do and how our Indigenous ancestors practiced something similar, strongly suggesting that the strong spirits of our ancestors have always guided us and continue to do so. With this remembrance, we root ourselves, trace, and reclaim our beauty and sacrality to our ancestors.

Whether you are reading this to learn about ancient Mesoamerican sacred ancestral veneration rites, to be hopefully moved by contemporary stories of ancestral connections, to be inspired and integrate curanderismo ancestral veneration rites, or to learn how to heal ancestral lineages, there is something here for you. As I always tell my clients, if there is something you need, do not obligate yourself to read or reread something in its entirety—go to the headings and get what your soul needs. Come back to it if and when you feel you can make the space and time to fully heal, integrate, or digest the information.

As I shared in my first book, *Cleansing Rites of Curanderismo*, in graduate school, I did not simply want to study the curanderx and become disassociated from my curanderismo practice. I am the curandera. I wanted to enact why these sacred practices are incredibly healing, nourishing for the soul, and absolutely transformative. As an attorney, yes, I worked on social justice cases, and my soul cried to provide justice beyond a box of typically limited monetary justice. So with the inspiration of my mentors and ancestors, I decided a long time ago to transition gradually and often painfully out of these roles. I became a politicized Xingona radical devotee of Nepantla spirituality, reclaiming myself for myself, and with my ancestors we move forward together in humility, compassion, pure faith, and absolute trust.

This book is my ofrenda (offering) to my ancestors and to you.

CHAPTER 1

Locating the Ancestors You Wish to Venerate

In some places around the world, many now have the opportunity to claim and openly identify with our ancestors, who may have been Indigenous, brujx (witches), curanderx, LGBTQ+ (Lesbian, Gay, Bisexual, Transexual, Queer, and beyond these categories), and many other historically marginalized ancestors. Privileges, especially for BIPOC (Black, Indigenous, and People of Color) and any group who has been historically marginalized, are often loaded with complex idiosyncrasies of having to fight for them in the first place. I am privileged to have been inspired by my parents, who were the first in their families to go to college to pursue a higher education. My Mexican father, an engineer who graduated from college in the States at sixteen, was ruthlessly and unjustly shot at work; this prompted his widow (my mother) to move us to the States and go to college herself. During our early years in the States, there were many times my mother was unsure what she would feed us, but I do not remember ever lacking. What I remember the most in my very early childhood was the immense adoration and pride I had for my mother. I wanted to mimic her, including the thrill of being able to join her and do my homework with her.

I gained a very high reading comprehension at a young age by hiding behind endless books—homework fabricated in an attempt to prevent many years of sexual molestation by the man my mother remarried. Reclaiming the most chastised parts of myself, the

Indigenous, in the face of varying degrees of familial disdain that erased my great-great-grandmother, who was a well-known curandera and well-versed in our Indigenous ways, inspired me to fight for my privilege to get a higher education and eventually bring to light our erased traditions and practices to popular audiences. Life's privileges, in and of themselves, should not be looked at as inherently bad. It is what we choose to do with our power and privilege that matters. I recognize my idiosyncrasies because my ancestors are rooted in them as well and, most importantly, I recognize my privilege, our privilege to reclaim and choose our ancestors.

This does not mean that our choices to identify with particular ancestors will go without scrutiny by those who want to maintain certain systems of oppression in place, especially the power to define and shape identities. Rather, it means that we continue to expand our freedoms as Xingonx, exercising them with respect, integrity, and honor. When we give someone else the power, right, and privilege to define our identity, we render away our power, rights, and privileges. The greatest forms of respect, integrity, and honor definitely include learning as much as we can about our ancestors and acknowledging them during this process. Whether the privilege and power to define who are our ancestors have come to us from a space of struggle or we have just simply always had this privilege, I hope that these Mesoamerican ancestral veneration practices inspire us to be mindful of this privilege and power to choose our ancestors, our roots, our identities, and that we do so with respect, honor, and integrity.

While it is important to keep in mind that deceased ancient Mesoamerican family members may have been loved and honored after their death, they may not have risen to the level of becoming an "ancestor" or possibly an "honorary ancestor." Unsurprisingly, royal and elite ancestors were afforded more elaborate funerary practices that enabled the continuation, renewal, and rebirth of their soul energy in more dynamic and eclectic ways. This practice does not necessarily indicate that all individuals actually perceived these royal and elite ancestors as having more ancestral prestige than their local, familial, or community ancestors or that they integrated a hierarchal system of distinguishing between certain types of ancestors.

The appropriation and negotiation of who they identified as an ancestor was connected to a myriad of complex diverse factors, including bestowed and associated rights, privileges, power, legitimization, and of course, a high degree of love and respect for them. They also appropriated ancestors that extended beyond blood relations. An ancestor could include an ancestor from the same or shared polity, local community, extended family, vocation, culture, and sacred land.

Ancient Mesoamericans' diverse funerary practices, traditions, and beliefs at the time of death provide rich insight as to who became an ancestor. The funerary rites described in this chapter were typically reserved for leaders and prominent members of a community and family—those that would be venerated and honored as ancestors.[1] The locations in which ancient Mesoamerican peoples buried their ancestors were essential to animating these spaces with the ancestor's soul energy, ensuring continued access to their ancestors, legitimatizing claims to positions and resources, and ensuring their rightful place in their afterlife.[2] They were also essential to ensuring their ancestor's agency in and access to cosmic creation, the nonordinary realms—Upperworld, Middleworld, and Underworld—and the realms of the living.

This chapter will first delve into the locations of their burials and the beliefs associated with them, as well as the likely practice and appropriation of foreign ancestors. We will explore the burial ancestral veneration practices that likely revealed who was deemed an ancestor, and we will draw from this ancient wisdom to explore who we choose to work with as our ancestor(s) as well as the curanderismo ceremonies that will enable us to connect with them.

ANCESTRAL BURIAL SITES OF ROYALS AND ELITES

Ancestral rulers and the elites were typically buried in shrines in the form of enormous temple structures or pyramids, and were often identified as ancestors of a polity or community.[3] In later periods, terminal Classic and Postclassic, these ancestors were often cremated rather than physically interred as they had been in the Classic period.[4] Whether it was through burial or cremation, the location of their burial sites was critical in procuring their role in cosmic creation and re-creation and access to the nonordinary realms, as well as the living planes.

These funerary temples were often constructed at locales and designed as cosmic mountains; each functioned as an axis mundi that allowed their ancestors to traverse the nonordinary realms and live alongside other esteemed ancestors, supernatural beings, and deities.[5] These grandiose public funerary temples also operated as a gigantic stage set to serve as the backdrop for huge processional rituals, dances, and offerings that bolstered the prestige of the ancestor. They also often had private spaces or caves of funerary altars, shrines, or sacred artwork for select people to access the power and sacrality of the ancestor in a more direct and profound level. The tomb of K'inich Janaab' Pakal I, in Classic-period Palenque, for example, had a small, elaborate, tube-like passage, a psychoduct that was built to connect the tomb of Pakal to the temple of the inscriptions with the outside, connecting the realms of the living and the dead.[6]

Envisioning and designing temples as sacred mountains and burying the remains of their ancestors within and underneath them went back to Central Mexico Teotihuacán and continued to Postclassic Tenochtitlan, wherein ancestors, deities, and other supernatural beings resided and could be accessed.[7] Because protecting the remains of their most esteemed ancestors was critical, actual cave inhumation was more theoretical than actual, as most caves could not be easily monitored and protected.[8] Elite funerary sites were placed in or near structures that symbolized sacred mountains that rose to the celestial floral paradisal realm.[9]

Cardinal funerary orientations were also critical in procuring the continuation, rebirth, and renewal of the soul energy of their ancestors and ensuring their continued agency and access. While there is considerable variability in the cardinal location of the funerary temple, its orientation, and the orientation of the body, were typically placed in the east or north or had an east–west or north–south orientation.

For many Classic and Postclassic Maya and Postclassic Central Mexican peoples, it was believed that the souls of royal ancestors, brave warriors, gods, and other supernatural beings came out of the East and traveled on the Flowery Road, the Sun's path, which ascended the levels of the Upperworld. The East was often conceived as the space of soul-giving energy of the rising Sun, rebirth, fertility, creation, and cyclical completion and renewal.[10] At the Maya Classic site of Caracol, eastern funerary temples frequently contain more than one formal interment.[11] At the Classic site of Río Bec, seventeen of the eighteen burials were oriented in an east–west direction.[12] At the Classic site of El Zotz, the Temple of the Night Sun and the Accession Platform are aligned perfectly along their centerlines, creating a clear link between two tombs and the individuals interred in them, who are buried at the west and east termini of the main axis of El Zotz.[13] The placing of individuals in an east–west orientation corresponded to their understanding of death as not just an end point, but as a cyclical cycle that entailed death and rebirth.[14]

The North was typically regarded as the space of ancestors, death, where the Sun reached its zenith, the direction of going up, the Upperworld and its realms, burgeoning life, ascension, and eminence.[15] The civic centers of Quiriguá, Tikal, Xunantunich, Piedras Negras, Palenque, and Copán had strongly marked north–south axes: the North housed royal tombs, funerary shrines, and sculpted monuments of esteemed ancestors, serving as allusions to their transition, perpetuation, rebirth, and resurrection. The long axes of royal graves were typically perpendicular to the solar path, usually with the head of the deceased pointing in a northerly direction.[16] North was associated with "up," the Sun God's "right" side, the heavens, the number thirteen, and the place of ancestors.

In the Classic city space of Tikal, important founding ancestors of the Tikal dynasties were interred on the northern side of the Great Plaza at the center of the city.[17] The funerary temple of Tikal's Sihyaj Chan K'awiil, Structure 33-1, is the tallest, grandest North Acropolis structure. It is a tomb in the sky where the ancestors resided and could be commemorated and accessed by the living, both publicly outside this grandiose temple and privately inside the temple by select heirs.[18]

Many royal Classic Maya also built chamber tombs for their ancestors within the architectural cores of pyramids and interrelated network of subterranean burial chambers.[19] Burying their ancestors within subterranean burial chambers was likely multilayered in purpose, including procuring their ancestor's influence over the Underworld—a space of decay and illness and potential renewal and rebirth within the womb of the Earth.[20] Subterranean burial chambers of elite esteemed ancestors were also found at Classic Teotihuacán and Postclassic Aztec structures.[21]

For the Postclassic Mexica, the North was the direction in which people went after they died and where it would be determined whether they would go to one of the Upperworld or the Underworld realms.[22] It was also a space where the Mexica buried the bodies or ashes of their ancestors.[23] The Great Temple of Tenochtitlan, Templo Mayor, dominated the landscape of the Mexica capital at 60 meters (197 feet) high. The north side was dedicated to Tlaloc, the rain god, while the southern half was the principal temple of the people's tutelary deity, Huitzilopochtli.

According to various sixteenth-century sources, the southern side of Templo Mayor symbolized the mythical mountain of Coatepec, the birthplace of Huitzilopochtli.[24] Templo Mayor and a courtyard adjoining the Templo, possibly Cu de Huichilobos, were where the cremation rituals of the most important figures of the Mexica elite took place. Cu de Huichilobos was one of the most revered spaces, as it was as believed to be located at the crossroads of the cardinal points and the planes of the universe.[25] Apart from two funerary urns recovered at the Templo Mayor that may contain the ashes of Mexica kings, no true royal burials have been excavated at Mexica sites.[26] Burying the cremated remains of the most important ancestors within the city-state's principal temple not only happened in Tenochtitlan, but also in other Postclassic Central Mexican polities like Texcoco.[27]

ANCESTRAL BURIAL SITES OF THE MIDDLE CLASS AND COMMONERS

Ancestral middle class and commoners were typically interred within residential courtyards and homes. This practice ensouled, animated, and nourished residential spaces with their ancestors' soul energies, prevented their bodies from being disturbed, aided ancestors in finding their way back to their living homes, enabled them to guide and protect those inhabiting the home(s), legitimized claims to inheritance or resources through genealogical ties, and served to symbolically record ancestry and descent lines.[28] Homes were often seen as both small-scale replicas of the cosmos and served as a trope—physical, symbolic, and linguistic—for the family.[29] Their interment within residential courtyards and homes facilitated their continued agency and roles in creation at cosmic, community, and familial levels. Communities and families also became the creators of their own ritualized relationship and access to their ancestors. The realm of the ancestors entailed community, that which is vocational, ceremonial, and familial—blood and extended family.[30]

At Teotihuacán, a huge multiethnic city-state with regional ties throughout Mesoamerica, bodies of ancestors were often buried within the household context, wherein ancestors still had an active role to play in life—giving credence to their descendant's social and spiritual positions.[31] Residential burial of their honorary deceased typically proclaimed and elevated them to ancestors, and proclaimed that in both life and in death, self, house, and community were important and interwoven expressions of identity.[32] The number of adults interred in the residential compounds was significantly smaller, relative to the area of each compound, indicating that not all deceased individuals made it to the rank of being an ancestor.[33]

While Teotihuacán foreigners were interred according to their specific cultural traditions—location, container, position, and funerary rites—foreigners, such as the Zapotec at the Oaxaca Barrio, Tlailotlacan, often adopted some of the Teotihuacán ancestral funerary practices.[34]

Teotihuacán residential apartment zones typically included spaces for food preparation and consumption, sleeping quarters, storage areas, sectors for refuse, courtyards for cult activities, and funerary areas.[35] Higher status ancestral veneration and funerary rites took place within the main courtyard of residential compounds and often accompanied the early construction phase of a high-end residential apartment compound.[36] Ancestors with families of lesser economic means were usually buried under floors of the house platforms or in nearby shrines.[37]

For the Maya, residential burials for the middle and lower ancestral classes were common in the Classic and Postclassic periods and continued even beyond the sixteenth-century Spanish conquest.[38] Ancestors often became a part of the physical foundation of the house, whether this was a stone foundation, a raised platform, or simply packed earth. Ancestors that had been buried in residences included both men and women.[39] In some sites, males were more commonly interred than females, but both were generally afforded the same burial treatment when interred.[40]

Data suggests that domestic interments often coincided with structural renovations, allowing the descendants to avoid issues that come about with the decomposition process.[41] At one of the oldest Maya sites, Dzibilchaltún (500 BCE to 1150 CE), new houses were built predominantly when an important member of the household died and were buried directly beneath the house walls or the surface of residential platforms.[42]

In Postclassic Central Mexico, the practice of residential burials continued for the ancestors of the middle class and commoners, with some nuances as to the manner in which they died. Building 3 at Tula Grande, the civic center of early Postclassic Tula, contains three main sectors—the West, Central, and East Groups—that feature houses with three steps that lead to and adjoin a sunken central courtyard with altars. The West Group Courtyard contains a human burial, an interred ancestor.[43] For the Postclassic Coastal Oaxaca Mixtec, residential burial of ancestors was an intrinsic part of the continuation and re-creation of community and individual identities that legitimized and imparted societal, economic, and spiritual claims to their descendants.[44]

The ashes of Mexica upper-middle ancestral classes were often placed within the interior of clay statues or urns, which were then interred in a deep hole near temples, at the summits of mountains, in shrines in the woods, and in the fields, courtyards, and chambers of their homes—keeping their ancestors close to community and familial spaces.[45] Burials were reserved for those who could not afford cremation, individuals from other territories, women who died in childbirth, and those called by Tlaloc—those who had died of drowning, lightning, leprosy, gout, or dropsy, and those that had been marked by the gods of rain and water. Women who died in childbirth were buried in the courtyard of the temple dedicated to the deity Cihuapipiltin and were deified as Cihuateteo warrior women who delivered the Sun from his daily zenith to the Underworld.[46]

Through residential burials, families became the creators and facilitators of their own relationship with their ancestors and ancestral veneration rites that continued to strengthen their connection to the sacred. They were in the constant presence of their ancestors. The selection of residential settings as final resting places facilitated ancestral processing and rituals, sustained familial rhythms, maintained communication with the living and their ancestors, and reinforced long-standing beliefs concerning the continuation, rebirth, and renewal of the ancestor's soul energy ensouling and animating residential spaces. Many of the burials that were found outside of the residence or residential courtyards lacked burial offerings or any preparations—suggesting that these individuals did not rise to the status of a would-be ancestor.[47]

MEXICA'S LIKELY APPROPRIATION OF FOREIGN ANCESTORS

While refashioning, reinventing, and claiming ties to ancestral lineages and identities to then bestow rights, privileges, and legitimize venerated roles and powers was a rather common occurrence among Mesoamerican peoples, the Mexica's constructed claim to their foreign

Teotihuacán and Toltec ancestors is particularly fascinating. There are distinctions as to where the Mexica migrated from in 1064, finally making their way to Tenochtitlan in 1273. Some show that they came from the desert lands of Aztlan or the seven caves of the land of Aztlan.[48] Codex Chimalpahin does not reference a desert; rather, it indicates that Aztlan was surrounded by a body of water. They crossed from boats to depart this island and landed at Culhuacan.[49] The records, however, all seem to agree that the Mexica were foreigners to the basin of Mexico, and came from very humble beginnings.

During their migration to Tenochtitlan, the records discuss their encounters with foreign tribes, including those then occupying Tula—the Chichimec and mountaineers—and discusses how they were continuously pushed out of foreign lands until they were divinely guided to the desolate marshy land of Tenochtitlan, a city-state that would be known for its unprecedented architectural beauty and cultural wonders.[50] Because they were resourceful and possessed prolific skills as warriors and sorcerers, they quickly climbed to power, and by the fifteenth century, they had formed a triple alliance with two other very powerful city-states, Texcoco and Tlacopan. But first Tlacopan, and then Texcoco, found their privileges and power diminishing under the unyielding pressure of the Mexica. By the beginning of the sixteenth century, their alliance with the Mexica was more honorary than actual.[51]

After the Mexica became more powerful, they claimed an ancestral connection to Teotihuacán and the Toltec and designed their ceremonial and administrative precinct, culture, customs, and mythologies to proclaim these connections. Their rulers went to Teotihuacán every twenty years to offer sacrifices and elected their hereditary rulers at Teotihuacán.[52] The Mexica, who lived in Tula, the capital and civic-ceremonial center of the Toltec, renovated some of the Toltec buildings, made public government-directed offerings there, and modeled some of their art and architecture after Tula prototypes.

Living in the capital of the Toltec from which they claimed ancestry was an effective way for the Mexica to absorb their history and culture, evident in countless examples of architecture and art in the Templo

Mayor, as their own.[53] The Mexica's appropriation of their foreign Toltec and Teotihuacán ancestors was nonetheless done with respect, honor, and integrity, in that they gave their cultural ancestors props by studying and recognizing them in their ceremonies, pilgrimages, and offerings.

CHOOSING OUR ANCESTORS

Distinguishing between an "ancestor" and an "honorary ancestor," wherein the latter identification may be reserved for those we work with more intimately or regularly in our different personal and familial healing and manifestation ceremonies, or having a hierarchical labeling of or relationship with our ancestors, is a personal choice. Many of my clients, especially my Xicanx clients, and myself may simply identify all of our deceased family members as ancestors and honor others as ancestors due to a cultural, land, or vocational sacred connection. For instance, on my ancestral altar, I have pictures that include my deceased family members and others I feel I have a sacred connection with. While I honor the memories of my deceased family members with daily copal ofrendas and identify them as my ancestors on my ancestral altar, I only work intimately with two of my deceased family members as ancestors in my ceremonies and trance journeys. But I identify all of them as my ancestors. I also have some clients who have hierarchical relationships and labeling systems of ancestors. Before we explore developing relationships with our ancestors, it is critical that we delve deeper into the understanding that choosing to develop these relationships is a power, right, and privilege, and again we should do so with respect, honor, and integrity.

Our path in establishing connections with our ancestors should ideally begin with first tuning into who we may feel connected to. Remember, we are not obligated to develop a relationship with and raise any of our deceased family members to ancestral status just because they are our blood or we share DNA with them. I have had clients share traumatizing stories about deceased grandparents or other family members that perpetrated or turned a blind eye to sexual and other kinds of atrocities within families. We may choose to offer those sides of our families healing and love, and if we sense it is right for us, we may honor their memory. At the same time, just as we are not required to develop an ancestral relationship with someone we do not feel a connection with, we may also be inspired, at different points of our lives, to start developing bonds with an ancestor we did not feel a connection to before.

There may also be occasions when an ancestor comes forward, and this ancestor is not part of our racial, ethnic, or cultural heritage, or we have been completely estranged from them. But we sense a strong connection to them; possibly they are an ancestor from a past life. If this happens, out of respect for everyone, do your due diligence and research what you can about them, especially if you intend to publicly claim them as part of your ancestral entourage. Do your research and see what feels intuitively right for you and whether the research you have encountered relates to this ancestor. If your connection is private and sweet, and you intend to keep it this way, this is also beautiful.

While appropriation is a fairly common dynamic throughout our histories and complex cultural developments, the taking of cultural practices without any recognition results in misappropriation. In this context, misappropriation of cultural practices takes place when the sources of inspiration are not recognized, especially when these sources come from or relate to historically marginalized peoples.

We want our ancestors to learn about us, know how we prefer to receive guidance, know ideal ways to intervene on our behalf, and so forth. Well then it only makes sense for us to learn what we can about them. If we have access to our elders, we can ask them, and also do our own personal research. With the internet making resources readily available and many academic sites making articles freely accessible, there is no excuse to not do our research and show our respect to our ancestors. Even if we have one-tenth of an ethnic or cultural lineage of a particular ancestor, it is out of respect, love, and honor that we do our research and due diligence.

If you would like to connect with ancestors outside of your blood lineage and they are part of a shared cultural identity, please also keep in mind that determining who they are and developing connections to them is truly an intuitive venture rather than an analytical one. Learn to trust what feels right and rings true for you. The more you trust and follow your intuitive intelligence, the stronger your intuition gets, as well as the connection with your ancestors. This connection can result in being blessed with their soul energy, healing, gifts, talents, and guidance.

LOCATING OUR ANCESTORS IN THE NONORDINARY REALMS

The nonordinary realms*—Upperworld, Middleworld, and Underworld—and the numerous spaces within these realms encompass the spirit and in-between realms wherein our ancestors can be accessed. For our ancient and some more contemporary Mesoamerican ancestors, each nonordinary realm was believed to have its own division and ordering; sacred gifts, insight, challenges, and medicine; and ancestors, deities, supernatural beings, and animals that were associated with one or more realms.

While elite and royal ancestors were typically associated with a Floral World in the Upperworld, being able to traverse, occupy, and obtain medicine, sacred gifts, and visions from all three realms was a highly prized skill that ancestors, especially previous rulers, were depicted as being able to master or realize. One of the most elegant and poignant demonstrations of this is the sarcophagus lid of ruler Pakal, which depicts his departure out of the Underworld and his ultimate resurrection, regeneration, and rebirth. The Underworld is depicted by the open maw of an infernal centipede. The resurrected ruler rises up

---

*The ancient Mesoamericans commonly divided the world into two forms: a quadripartite form that was horizontally organized into four cardinal spaces (East, West, North, and South) with a center in the middle, and a tripartite form, that was a vertical division of the nonordinary realms into the Underworld, Middleworld, and Upperworld. The Middleworld encompassed the cardinal spaces.[54]

along a World Tree, which acts as an axis mundi or portal that transfers his body to the Floral Paradise of the Upperworld.[55] The nine lords of the Underworld are depicted in stucco reliefs on the walls of his tomb. In the space between his tomb and the temple above, there are thirteen vaults representing the thirteen levels of the Upperworld he is ascending into.[56]

The soul energy of our beloved ancestors, especially ones that have a stronger degree of soul energy, will be able to guide us to and through these realms when we need medicine, messages, or insight from them and aid us in bringing back medicine for ourselves, family, and loved ones. Because our ancestors may appear in different nonordinary realms in our journey work with them, it is helpful to be able to discern the symbolism, medicine, and common terrain of these realms. Being aware of these factors will also help us to discern messages, medicine, and guidance they have for us, as well as help us to strengthen our connections to our ancestors.

While our ancestors were believed to reside in the Floral Paradise of the Upperworld, our ancestors could also traverse and reside in the other nonordinary realms. I often find ancestors during a journey with a client at a particular nonordinary realm because they are looking after my client's lost soul piece(s), would like my client to connect with a particular gift or medicine of that nonordinary realm, or they are obtaining medicine, gifts, or insights from these realms for themselves, family, lineage mentees, or us in these realms. Let yourself be open, humble, and grateful about what you are shown in your journeys and in connecting with your ancestors in these realms. The more we do this, the more our ancestors will come to us to aid, guide, and intervene on our behalf.

Upperworld

For the ancient Mesoamerican peoples, the Upperworld was typically linked with the sky and cosmos. It was where animating energy was stored and emitted and a space that could be observed for divinatory purposes to better understand the activities of the deities, ancestors, and supernatural beings, and to discern when to perform certain rituals. The Upperworld was also where the idealized processes of rebirth and resurrection took place. The Upperworld of the ancient Mesoamericans was often divided into thirteen ascending levels, although a few Postclassic Central Mexican sources indicate a division of nine or twelve.[57] Each level reflected and emitted a different aspect of soul energy.[58]

Vatican Codex A describes the various levels of the Central Mexican Upperworld. The lowest one was the one that was visible to all. It was the realm where the Moon and clouds traveled. The second level was Citlalco, the place of the stars.[59] The third level was the one in which Tonatiuh, the Sun deity, resided.[60] The fourth was Ihuicatl Hhuitztlan, the place where Venus (Citlalpol) could be seen. The fifth was the level of the comets, the smoking stars or meteors (*citlalin popoca*), an immediate source of tonalli. The sixth and seventh levels were the levels of night and day, where only the colors green and blue could be seen (or alternatively, black and blue). The eighth level was the place of storms. The ninth, tenth, and eleventh were the dwelling place for the gods. The twelfth and thirteenth comprised Omeyocan, the place of duality, the source of generation and life, the primordial dwelling place of their principal creator deity, Ometeotl.[61]

Ethnohistorical codices and artwork provide further insight into some of the paradisal realms of the Upperworld. Tlalocan (place of Tlaloc), the fourth layer of the Upperworld, was an earthly paradise of green plants and unending springtime. Those who died from phenomena associated with water, such as lightning, drowning, and waterborne diseases, went to Tlalocan.[62] The Flower World, Xochitlan or Tonatiuhilhuicac was another paradisal realm, where esteemed ancestors would become birds and butterflies and spend an eternity drinking the nectar of flowers in this heavenly realm and on Earth.[63] Chichihualcuauhco was another paradisal realm, where the souls of dead children went. It was the place of a celestial nursemaid tree, which had breasts hanging from it and children drinking from it.[64]

The thirteen ascending levels of the Maya Upperworld were

associated with different planets, deities, comets, and the Sun. Although the specific dynamics of these thirteen levels are not yet fully understood, their artwork and the *Books of Chilam Balam*** provide insight on these thirteen levels. According to the *Chilam Balam of Maní,* the Moon was in the first, the stars were in the second, Venus was in the third, the Sun and Mercury were in the fourth, Mars was in the fifth, and Jupiter and Saturn were in the sixth levels. The *Chilam Balam of Kaua* placed Venus in the third and the Sun in the fourth level.[65] In artwork, the Sun and Moon were often depicted along a double-headed serpent that represented the ecliptic and traced the annual motion of the Sun across the sky.

Diego de Landa, a sixteenth-century missionary and ethnographer, mentions that the Yucatec Maya conceived of a paradisal realm, where those that led a virtuous life would enter this realm free of pain, where there was an abundance of food, delicious drinks, and a refreshing and shady tree called the *yaxché* (ceiba) tree, under which they could rest and be in peace forever.[66] De Landa does not say whether this paradisal realm was in the Upperworld. Karl Taube, Mesoamerican scholar, points out that this paradisal realm is likely Flower World or Flower Mountain. The Flower World was ubiquitous in Maya art: it was both the dwelling place of ancestors and the mode in which ancestors and celestial gods ascended into the sky.[67] In architecture, Flower World was portrayed as a pyramid with stairways often flanked with plumed serpents, which likely served as a symbolic passage into this paradisal Upperworld. Flower World was also associated with the East, at the dawning of the Sun, and the North, when the Sun was at its zenith.[68] Hence, Flower World was not necessarily stationary in the sky: it followed the path of the Sun and was likely one of the most revered Upperworld realms.

---

*The *Books of Chilam Balam* are the sacred books of the Maya of Yucatán; they are the most important source on the traditional knowledge of the early colonial Maya as written information from this period is rather sparse. They were handwritten and are named after the small towns where they were originally kept.

Terrain and Medicine of the Upperworld

Please keep in heart and mind that my description of the nonordinary realms and the medicines they offer should not be interpreted as the final say about these realms; rather, they are provided as guidelines. You can use them as a springboard and soar with them or just flow with your intuitive insight.

In my personal experiences and those of my mentors and clients, the Upperworld tends to involve cosmic, magical, and surreal terrains, feels weightless and soft, and appears ethereal. I have seen the inner children of my clients riding on feathered serpents, being counseled by esteemed ancestors, playing among singing flowers, and have seen castles and temples made of beautiful crystals and minerals. The Upperworld can be entered through dreams, mountain caves, tree trunks, waterfalls, and visualizations of clouds or rainbows.

The gifts and medicines of the Upperworld include:

- Obtaining guidance, intervention, or aid from ancestors or other divine supernatural (earthly and cosmological) beings.
- Tapping into the sacred energies of rebirth, resurrection, and creation.
- Connecting with childlike innocence, bliss, joy, and happiness.
- Charging items and spaces with particular planetary or star energies, and accessing sacred essence energies from the Sun and the cardinal spaces.

Another gift of the Upperworld is the ability to connect with and retrieve soul pieces. Pieces of our soul that are in the Upperworld are usually there to obtain medicine for something for which the truth is too difficult to see or because someone or something we held up on a pedestal let us down.

Middleworld

The Middleworld was composed of the four cardinal spaces and a center as well as natural and constructed spaces that acted as portals to access the sacred energies of the cardinal spaces and the nonordinary realms; it also provided doorways and homes for ancestors, deities, and supernatural beings to enter or reside. The cardinal spaces could be fixed—like our notion of four fixed points, which can be determined by a compass—but they could also be seen as diverse movements and categories where and when a specific process took place.[69] As David Stuart, Mesoamerican scholar, points out, there was likely a variety of forms and ideas concerning the cardinal spaces, whether they were expressed in the shape of a quincunx or in some other form. With the quincunx, for example, the movements could encompass the solstitial points, marking the yearly movement of the Sun along the Earth's horizon and the center, but it could also represent the points of sunrise and sunset and zenith and nadir—the processes and locations of the daily movement of the Sun around the Earth.[70]

The cardinal spaces were also sacred entities in their own right. They each had their own forms of divine wisdom, sacred gifts, patrons, colors, World Trees, deities, day signs, year signs, and mountains, and their symbols, meanings, and purposes often varied among the ancient Mesoamericans. The sacred entities of the cardinal spaces were also responsible for the elements—fire, sun, water, air, and earth—that maintained equilibrium on Earth.[71] Each one of the cardinal spaces was believed to store and emit soul energy and had a World Tree that acted as an axis mundi where the nonordinary realms could be accessed.[72] Shamans traveled to these other worlds to diagnose and cure ailments, to access supernatural wisdom and medicine, and to retrieve soul pieces.[73]

Ancestors could occupy sacred geological features of the landscape, such as mountains, caves, forests, particular trees, ravines, anthills, edges of volcanoes, certain bodies of water, and at intersections between two natural elements. They also dwelled in buildings and architectural spaces that mirrored sacred natural spaces and acted as portals to the Upperworld and Underworld.

The Middleworld also comprised parallel Earth realms, both temporal and spatial. Shaman soothsayers accessed these parallel realms by seeing into a past or present event. They could also go into the crevices of a crossroad or into an anthill to recover someone's lost ton-alli.[74] Research on dreams and dream interpretation by the sixteenth-century ethnographer Friar Bernardino de Sahagún in his work *Primeros memoriales* (*First Memorials*) also suggests that traveling to other realms during dreams via the tonalli included parallel Earth realities of the Middleworld at different times and places. Sahagún's material on dream interpretation includes dreams of people at some future time or parallel reality, where they are seeing their homes burn down, singing in their homes, or building new homes, all reflecting parallel Middleworld realms.[75]

Terrain and Medicine of the Middleworld

The Middleworld is parallel with Earth realms and tends to look like literal or metaphorical places on Earth. All of the Earth's times and histories can be accessed in the Middleworld. The space-times are holograms, so time can be stopped to inspect and examine something further to understand, honor, and integrate lessons. The Middleworld can be entered through dreams, mountain caves, tree trunks, and our memories of an "earthly" location.

Some of the common gifts and medicines of the Middleworld:

- Connect with and/or retrieve soul pieces. Pieces of our soul that are in the Middleworld are usually residing there to obtain medicine for something that happened in another point in our life or a past life.
- Tap into sacred energies of fertility, renewal, and creation of life.
- Learn how to be resilient and change with greater ease and grace.
- Gain access to bounty and abundance.
- Heal, rescript, and shift a situation that happened in our current life or a past life.
- Ground and balance ourselves energetically, mentally, physically, and emotionally.
- Gain wisdom from the Earth and its elements.

Underworld

The Underworld was typically understood as a dreaded place of tests and tribulations and was associated with darkness, the night, the Night Sun, and the Moon. At the same time, it harbored regenerative powers and at night emitted transformative energies. It was believed that the Sun deity journeyed into the Underworld at night, shapeshifted into a jaguar, and resurrected at dawn once again.[76] Interestingly, many planets, deities, and natural phenomena had nocturnal and diurnal aspects, wherein they journeyed into and transformed and became lords and residents of the Underworld at night. Ancestors, deities, and supernatural beings also traversed and resided in the Underworld.

The Central Mexican peoples believed that the Underworld was comprised of nine levels, eight of them below the earth. Most people who died of natural causes, diseases, accidents, or other circumstances not specified by the gods inhabited the Underworld.[77] In their human creation myth *Leyenda de los soles* (Legend of the Suns), Quetzalcoatl, a deity of creation and wind, was required to journey into the Underworld to retrieve the bones of humans from the previous world. The devious Mictlantecuhtli, the principal lord of the Underworld, agreed to give up the bones but required Quetzalcoatl to undergo tests, which included blowing music from a solid conch shell. With the help of some worms and bees, he successfully passed the tests, obtained the bones, and ran off with them. Eventually Quetzalcoatl returned the bones to Tamoanchan, the place of origin, where Cihuacoatl, a Mother Earth deity, ground them into a flourlike meal on which the gods then shed drops of their blood to create the present race of humans. Due to Quetzalcoatl's success in passing the tests of the Underworld, new life and beginnings were forged.[78]

The Maya believed that the Underworld consisted of nine levels beneath the earth. The entrance to the Underworld was a watery place that could be entered at the crossing of two rivers, through caves, bodies of standing water, and dark, wild places, such as forests.[79] In the K'iché' Maya Postclassic text, *Popol Vuh,* the Underworld is depicted as a watery realm or an actual body of water and as a source of transformation and resurrection. The mythical Hero Twins go through a series of tests that appear to be metaphors for overcoming illness and death. As a ploy to trick the Underworld lords, the bones of the twins are ground up like cornmeal and then thrown into a river. The faith and heroic deeds of the Hero Twins are rewarded, and they are resurrected as handsome boys and eventually defeat the lords of the Underworld.[80]

Terrain and Medicine of the Underworld

The Underworld can resemble earthlike terrains, including oceans, seas, mountains, forests, bridges, jungles, and caves. It is typically volatile and can melt away into something else at the blink of an eye, especially as we go into deeper self-awareness and pass our trials and tribulations. The inhabitants of the Underworld are typically described as the spirits of plants, animals, elementals, and beings known as Earthkeepers. Earthkeepers know the vast multidimensional and intradimensional nature of Earth and can grant access to any earthly plane, reality, or time. They can help us traverse more than one reality at one time. Our ancestors and animal guides can lead us through the Underworld and take us to the Earthkeepers. It is typical to enter the Underworld through a pool of water or through some opening such as a cave, tree trunk, cenote, or tunnel.

Some of the gifts and medicine of the Underworld include:

- Absorb its regenerative powers if we do indeed move forward with releasing toxic energies weighing us down.
- Take advantage of the transformative energies it emits at night.
- Allow it to inspire persistence, courageousness, and humility.
- Understand, work with, and heal our shadow aspects.
- Connect with and retrieve soul pieces. Understand what we need to release, so we can welcome back home our lost soul pieces.

JOURNEYING THROUGH THE SACRED HEART

Our sacred heart is the space where we can safely journey to the non-ordinary realms, as well as to all dimensions, soul lineages, worlds, and realities—past, present, and future. Malina, one of my mentors, taught me to journey by going through *el sagrado corazón* or the sacred heart. She explained that it was deep within the heart. It is the space where we are the "I Am" presence, the divine presence within all of us, and we become and have access to infinite possibilities. Journeying within the sacred heart helps us release and transmute duality consciousness, fear, doubt, and other lower-vibration thoughts and emotions. It also encourages us to remember our infinite nature and inspires us to reclaim our power to create ideal realities for ourselves.

For ancient Mesoamerican peoples, the heart of a place, space, sacred object, or person could be synonymous with the axis mundi, where sacred energy converges and permits access to the nonordinary realms.[81] The central axis of the universe was often portrayed as a World Tree that acted as a cosmic bridge for the nonordinary realms; its roots were deep in the Underworld, its trunk was in the Middleworld, and its branches reached the Upperworld. The World Tree, as the central axis, was mirrored at each of the other cardinal spaces—South, West, North, and East—each with its own distinct tree and bird. These other World Trees, seen as the four corners of the sky, could also act as bridges between worlds.[82]

It is these realms where we can greatly deepen the connection with our ancestors. There is, however, a paradox in this journey; there is no entering or journeying into the sacred heart. Rather, we are simply remembering that there is no separation between us and the divine and that we embody the divine. In this divine remembrance, "protection" from others is no longer needed on any level. As the divine, we choose what we allow into our space. We can simply set the intention of what we choose and know that this intention will hold. Nonetheless, the ritual of journeying into the sacred heart always inspires deep humility, compassion, and love within me, and so I always engage in this ceremony. I love it and hope you will too.

Space Limpia Before Your Journey

Whether or not you engage in the recommended breathwork exercises, before journeying into the sacred heart to connect with an ancestor, please consider cleaning up and doing a space limpia for the space where you will be engaging in your journey work to set the stage and ensure that the energy around you is balanced and clean. I cover many different ways to do space limpias in *Cleansing Rites of Curanderismo,* and an easy way to cleanse your space is to smudge* it with a dry bundle of herbs, such as sage, rosemary, cedar grass, or sweetgrass—all herbs have cleansing properties. You can also do a white fire limpia. For a white fire limpia you will need:

- A pot with a handle, preferably a stainless steel or cast-iron pot. (The tools you use for limpias should never be used for actual cooking, eating, or drinking. They are your sacred magical items and should be placed in a separate space, out of reach, so they are not mistakenly used.)
- A couple of handfuls of plain Epsom salts.
- Approximately 8 to 10 tablespoons of rubbing alcohol (a small splash).
- Dry plants. Any one or a combination of them is excellent to clear, feed, and revitalize spaces: rosemary, rue, lemongrass, sage, parsley, lavender, chamomile, tobacco, lantana flowers.

You can set the pot down on the ground, or you can carefully hold it by the handle, depending on what you feel comfortable with. Place all of the items in the pot. Before the white fire limpia, please thank the spirits of the fire and herbs for helping you cleanse your living space. If you feel comfortable, please also consider thanking all the items used for this limpia and all of your limpias. The items used in our limpias are believed to have a spirit and so we thank them before working with them. Then carefully throw a lit wooden match into the pot. Once the space has been cleansed, engage in the recommended shamanic breathwork (optional) and trance journey into the sacred heart to access an ancestor.

---

*Smudging is a cleansing method that requires getting a bundle of dried herbs, lighting them, and gently waving the bundle around your body, sacred items, and living spaces to cleanse and bless them with the smoke coming from the bundle.

Sacred Heart Connection with an Ancestor

Listening to recordings of repetitive rhythmic drumbeats, binaural beats, crystal bowls, and Hemi-Sync music may help to access trance or deep meditative states. In my classes and work with clients, I like to use a combination of sound, breathwork, and stimulation of energy centers. But depending on how easily you can access trance or deep meditative states, you may or may not need to engage in the recommended shamanic breathwork exercises. Various types of shamanic breathwork exercises can induce particular trance states. Some can calm and quiet the monkey mind, while others can give us a restorative energy that enables us to journey into the nonordinary realms. Following are shamanic breathwork exercises I feel are ideal for this work.

Breathwork to Journey into the Sacred Heart to Connect with an Ancestor

◈ Centering Breathwork Exercise

Cup your hands over face, take a big inhale, and hold your breath for a few seconds. Before exhaling place your hands in a prayer position and slowly exhale while moving your hands down while still in prayer position. As you move your hands down, set the intention of aligning all of your energy to the center of the chest, our energy center of unconditional love, forgiveness, and compassion. Repeat three times.

◈ Activating the Energy Center of the Heart

Position your hands in the raising Maya mudra:* Curl in the index, middle, ring, and pinky fingers to the first digit and place these curled-in fingers against the center of the chest while keeping your thumb straight. Inhale, then exhale with an "ah." Repeat three times.

---

*Mudras are hand, body, or facial postures that act as catalysts for speeding up electromagnetic currents and affect the subtle energy bodies. Like acupressure points, they stimulate particular areas and correlating energetic systems that enable us to go into specific nonordinary realms.

◈ Balancing into Higher Consciousness

Inhale, hold your breath, and tighten all of the muscles in your buttocks and lower and upper abdomen, slightly curling in the spine. Hold your breath for about 30 seconds and envision a ruby ball of energy forming at your tailbone. Exhale slowly out of the mouth and allow the ruby ball to travel up the spine, slowly straightening the spine, and bring the ruby ball up to the top of the head. Repeat three times.

◈ Trance Journey into the Sacred Heart to Connect with an Ancestor

While taking slow and intentional inhales and exhales, take a moment and contemplate whether there is a specific ancestor you would like to connect to. Alternatively, you can remain open as to the ancestor, and consider whether you are called to connect with: a blood relation, extended family, a cultural or vocational connection, or an ancestor associated with a particular region of the world you feel intuitively connected to.

Allow yourself to go into a trance or meditative state through intention or any of the above recommended methods. Take a moment or two to acknowledge yourself for taking the time and space to do something that could nourish and nurture your spirit and soul, and permit your heart to continue to open up to you. Set the intention of journeying into your sacred heart and connecting with the divine presence within you, your I Am. If you are having trouble connecting with your I Am, a powerful and effective method for entering this space is both a command and a statement of truth: "Stand aside, ego, in the name of God.* I Am That I Am."

Allow your heart to continue to open up to you and love yourself even more. As you open your heart, imagine an emerald light streaming out from the center of your chest. At the other side of the emerald light is a mirror reflection of you; it is the you that always attracts ideal synchronicities

---

*I use the term *God* to mean "divine love," free of any religious association. If you are not comfortable with the term God, use a word or concept that signifies pure divinity and consciousness to you.

in your life, the you that knows how to and does manifest in and with impeccability, the you that is pure love and only love.

Now see your I Am become infinitely small, standing on a zero-point stream of light radiating from your sacred heart. Walk toward and into the sacred heart. The first gateway into the sacred heart is the violet fires of transfiguring divine love and infinite physical perfection. Allow the violet fires to completely encompass, caress, and love you. Place into it any toxic emotions or beliefs that you are ready to let go of, especially self-judgment, self-criticism, fears, and doubts. Allow yourself to remain in the violet fires throughout this journey, releasing stuff that you are ready to let go of, as well as things that may come up in the journey. We are multidimensional within the sacred heart. The second gateway into the sacred heart is the white fires of purification and resurrection. Allow the white fires to also completely encompass, caress, love, and inspire you to remember and become your infinite I Am nature.

Before stepping out of the white fires, set the intention of going to the nonordinary realm where the ancestor you are open to or choosing to connect with is currently located or is willing to meet you. Step out of the sacred heart and take a moment to tune into the nonordinary realm where you are. Allow a light of love to shine out from the center of your chest and use it to communicate with your ancestor. Once again, softly refocus on the ancestor you would like to connect to, whether it be a specific blood ancestor, any blood ancestor, extended family, a cultural or vocational connection, or an ancestor associated with a particular region of the world you feel intuitively connected to. Let the ancestor know the reasons you would like to connect with them.

If an ancestor appears, and if it feels in alignment for you, ask them to share any or all of the following:

- their stories with you
- what connects the two of you
- what messages they have for you
- if they have something to teach or share with you
- if there is anything they need from you

- if they would like to receive healing from you or experience healing with you
- if they would help you connect with a gift or medicine from the nonordinary realm where they appeared to you
- to guide you through and teach you about this nonordinary realm
- anything else you may be guided to ask them

Please give them an opportunity to share whatever they would like, and lovingly listen and hold space for them. Offer them an ofrenda for sharing their wisdom with you. This could encompass a crystal, cacao, a brightly colored feather, corn, flowers—whatever you intuitively feel is appropriate. Consider a gift that is high in soul energy to continue to strengthen their soul energy. Pretty much anything that grows with the aid of the Sun or gets charged by the Sun usually has strong soul energy. In addition, birds with brightly colored feathers, such as hummingbirds, parrots, macaws, quetzal, lovely cotinga, and toucans were believed to flash like fire in the bright sunlight and give off soul energy.[83]

If you are unsure of whether an ancestor appeared, throw this uncertainty into the violet fires and please remain open, humble, and in gratitude for their aid, guidance, and intervention. Keep in mind that oftentimes our clairvoyant (psychic vision) gifts may need to be cultivated a little or a lot more until we see them in our mind's eye. They may also come through other developed intuitive gifts, such as claircognizance (psychic knowing), clairaudience (psychic hearing), clairsentience (psychic feeling), clairalience (psychic smell), and clairgustance (psychic tasting), so again please be open, humble, and grateful, and you will continue to open the doors of perception with higher emotional frequencies of faith and trust. There are numerous ways to develop these gifts, and one very simple and practical way to develop each psychic gift is to exercise our imagination focusing on each sixth sense. If we can imagine it, then in some reality or dimension it exists; it is just a matter of fine-tuning which reality or dimension you choose to tune into. If it feels in alignment with you, assume that they are with you, ask them any or all of the above questions, and use your light of love from your heart to communicate with them.

Before leaving this nonordinary realm, thank them for continuing to guide you as the days, weeks, and months unfold. Then see yourself being reborn first in the sacred white fires of purification and resurrection and then in the violet fires—seeing the violet-fire angels congratulating you for being vulnerable, brave, and bold, and releasing that which no longer served you. Then take six deep breaths, inhaling through the nose and exhaling out through the mouth. Gently rub your thighs with your hands, coming back fully present and grounded.

After the journey, please consider creating an ancestral altar, even if it is a small table, space, or one that is being slightly or greatly refashioned. We will discuss creating ancestral altars in the second chapter.

RITES TO STRENGTHEN ANCESTRAL CONNECTIONS AFTER AN INITIAL OR EARLY CONNECTION

It is common to sense a stronger connection to certain ancestors or discover other ancestors at different points in our lives. Whether or not we are fully aware of it, many of us are constantly in the process of discovering what we love, what makes us happy, and defining and redefining our identities, so it is not surprising that we would resonate with particular ancestors at different points in our lives. It is also a beautiful practice to occasionally tune in and see if an additional ancestor has come forward to connect, heal, and grow with us.

We will, of course, cover numerous ways to continue to develop our connections with our ancestors, and these suggested rites are for ancestors in the earlier stages of our relationship with them. Remember these rites can be for a specific ancestor you would like to work with, or you can remain open as to the ancestor, and in this fluid space consider whether you are called to connect with a blood relation, extended family, a cultural or vocational connection, or an ancestor associated with a particular region of the world you feel intuitively connected to.

The Gift

Place a representation of the gift you offered them in your trance journey or a gift you are intuitively guided to give them. Take a moment to engage in some deep breathing and set the intention of allowing a light of love to shine out from your heart. Through this light of love offer your ancestor this gift and place it next to your bed, on your altar (this can be any altar, including an ancestral altar), or some place special.

If you are unsure what kind of representation you should use, again, please consider offering something that holds a high degree of soul energy. Our ancestors are soul energy, and through this gift your ancestor will have a way to access you more readily in this third-dimensional plane.*

Placement of Their Image or Something that Represents Them

There will be times we have pictures of our ancestors, and there will be many times we do not have access to their images, for many different reasons, so please tune into something you feel represents them. Leave this image or something that represents them next to your bed, on your altar (this can be any altar, including an ancestral altar), or some place special. This can include having a picture of a sacred land or site, an image of a particular period you associate with them, or an imaginary place you associate with them. Please do not push or rush this connection; let it flow with ideal ease and grace.

When I first began making ancestral connections with curandera María Sabina (1894–1985), who worked in the Mazatec tradition of healing, divination, and soul retrieval work with psylocibin mushrooms, I read *María Sabina: Selections* and watched any and all videos I could find of her. In one journey, she was saying one of her poems to me in a melodic tone. Shortly thereafter, I adapted one of her poems into a medicine song and began singing it at our sound bath ceremonies. After honoring her through my prayers, song, gratitude, and copal, she came

---

*Items that usually have strong soul energy are listed in the exercise on page 43.

to me and told me that we were family and that we understood how to work and heal with the santos, the mushrooms. I knew at that point she had become one of my honorary cultural ancestors.

A couple of weeks later, one of my clients gave me a beautiful painted portrait of María Sabina. I feel she knew that despite our growing connection, I was still too shy to include her image on my ancestral altar and identify her as one of my cultural ancestors. This client shared with me that he found the portrait in a little shop in Tulúm, Mexico, hidden on the floor. The portrait called out to him, and he knew it was meant for me. I am tearing up writing this because this doubt, shyness, and feelings of unworthiness happen to so many of us. But thank goodness, our ancestors also find a way to strengthen their connection with us.

When I received the portrait, I immediately placed María Sabina in the center of my ancestral altar with beautiful wooden mushrooms that had also been gifted to me in front of her. I know María Sabina was the one who taught me to open up to ancestors that extended beyond my bloodline. I am incredibly grateful and humbled by her teachings.

So again, I cannot stress the importance of being patient with the development of our ancestral connections. Oftentimes, making these connections can be healing for us, which is usually a process in and of itself. Let it happen with ideal ease and grace.

🎐 Writing a Love Letter

Allow yourself to get in a relaxed meditative or trance state with breathwork—deep inhales and exhales—or simply set the intention of getting into this state. Write a love letter to your ancestor, and if this resonates with you, in the letter explain to them:

- why you would love to have an ancestor guiding, aiding, and intervening on your behalf
- how you would love for them to communicate with you
- a message you feel they gave you

- why you perceive a connection to them
- what you would love to learn from them
- how you would love for them to teach you
- anything else you feel is necessary or relevant

Next to the letter, leave an open bottle of your favorite essential oil or fragrant flowers, or keep an oil diffuser running next to the love letter. Rather than eating actual food, many contemporary Yucatec Maya acknowledge breath, wind, and sweet-smelling fragrances are not only the food for ancestors and spirits, but they also constitute their spiritual nature. These sweet-smelling fragrances will attract your ancestor to your love letter. Please consider leaving this love letter on your altar, next to your bed, or in some other place that is special to you.

Sharing Food and Drink

Bring the picture or something that represents your ancestor to the dining table. Invite them to come and eat with you and possibly your family to prepare a plate and glass of whatever you are having for them. A nice touch is to fan the smell of the food or drink with a bird feather or feather fan as an offering and request that the feather(s) carry the aroma into the nonordinary realms. Once you have given them space and time to arrive and ideally before the food gets cold, take your first bite and then begin to share anything you feel is important to strengthen your connection with your ancestor. Once your conversation is complete, depending on your compost and food, place the food and drink in your compost or bury it. I also leave a glass of water on my ancestral altar and change it weekly.

Please keep in mind that this shared food and drink is believed to take on the soul energy of our ancestor. It is tradition to have our ancestors also become a part of our rich nutrient soil that nourishes our vegetables, fruit, herbs, and our gardens in general. It is a recycling, rebirth, and renewal of sacred ancestral soul energy. We will explore much more about this recycling, rebirth, and renewal of soul energy in chapters four and five.

Make Daily or Weekly Offerings of Copal, Resin, or Incense

Make daily, weekly, or monthly ofrendas a part of a normal routine. I make offerings as part of my morning work week and before I go for my morning run. If you work it into your routines, it is easier to remember to do it regularly. Lighting a charcoal tablet to place copal or some other resins on it or lighting an incense stick only takes a couple of minutes; it is the remembering part that can be tricky. When make an offering of copal, place the charcoal tablet on a steel brazier or urn or on a glazed *popoxcomitl* (copalero), or censer. But if we make it part of a routine, it becomes easier to remember. My ancestors love copal, so this is what I use. Start with a scent you love. Normally your ancestors will also love it.

CHAPTER 2

Invocations That Welcome Ancestors into Our Lives

The first time in my life I finally and felt truly connected to my father was when I created a very public multilayered altar for my father for *El día de los muertos* (Day of the Dead) in the front of my house in my early thirties. Throughout all of my life speaking about my father was taboo. I was only two years old when he was shot, so for some reason it was presumed that I could not have been traumatized by the loss of a good, loving father in my life. The little I was told of him was that he was a very generous, loving, and thoughtful man. He wanted me to call him by his first name, so I would think of him as a friend, first and foremost. Apparently, he had a contentious relationship with his father and did not want to repeat this cycle with me and hoped we would be good friends. I knew his death was incredibly painful for my mother, so I never really felt safe to ask her about him. The man that my mother later remarried sadly took every opportunity he could to speak poorly about my deceased father, so it became another reason to stay quiet. I mourned for my father's death in silence for most of my upbringing. When I became an adult, I began my journeys of deep healing and created spaces to openly reclaim my culture and my father.

It was the first time I had ever celebrated El día de los muertos, and I decided to do with it a bang. Instead of the Halloween decorations that adorned the front of my neighbor's yards, I created a large, multi-layered altar for my father and placed it in my front yard. Before then, I spent many weekends hand-painting and decorating picture frames for my father alonside numerous other beautiful and colorful related crafts that are left for our families on these altars. My mother helped me one Sunday when I expressed to her that this is what I would be doing and she was welcome to join. She did, and for one of the first times in my life, I felt safe to ask about him in the context of what she thought he would like for his altar. During the three days of El día de los muertos, I cooked my father's favorite foods and placed them, along with his favorite beverages and hundreds of marigolds, on his altar. The front of my house and lawn also had dancing skeletons, inviting my father to celebrate, eat, drink, and dance. Through these offerings I created and reclaimed a space to begin to truly reconnect with him and finally welcome him in my life, and many years later he became one of my beloved ancestors.

In creating our own altars, we can reflect on the offerings the ancient Mesoamericans left for their ancestors at their altars—funerary sites, public and private shrines, and tables. While these offerings were multilayered in meaning and purpose, they helped them to ensure a strong connection with their ancestors. The offerings provided comfort, aid, nourishment, and guidance to their ancestors, so they might successfully navigate the worlds of the afterlife. They could procure an ancestor's continuation, rebirth, and renewal of soul energy into some other form, place, or role, and they were also a means by which ancestors and the living could commune and connect with one another. These offerings could successfully invoke their ancestor's aid, guidance, legitimization, and intervention. While I will discuss these aspects separately, they typically overlapped in purpose and meaning.

In this chapter, I will explore the sacred offerings the ancient Mesoamericans used to venerate and strengthen their connections with their ancestors to then use this knowledge to inform the creation of our ancestral altars, where to place them in our homes, and how to clean and cleanse our spaces and altars, and I will also discuss how to care for and enliven the sacred items we place on our ancestral altars with our ancestor's sacred soul energies. I will also share how the creation of one of my client's ancestral altars not only strengthened the connection with her ancestors, but how bringing sacred items from her ancestral altar to her place of work resulted in a more tranquil workspace.

OFRENDAS THAT PROVIDED COMFORT AND PRESTIGE

Ancestors were often depicted in quatrefoil cartouches that materialized portals between human and ancestral worlds, conveying their understanding that ancestors inhabited a realm parallel to the human world.[1] Various kinds of items left at funerary sites—jewelry, clothing, ceramic vessels, shells, precious stones, food, copal, figurines, and much more—were offerings that could be accessed and used by their ancestors to ensure their comfort in the nonordinary realms of the afterlife.

Teotihuacán burials of various classes were accompanied by ceramic vessels, censers, mica, slate, obsidian, and shells—and, of course, the wealthier the ancestor, the more items were offered to provide their ancestors comfort in the nonordinary realms of the afterlife.[2] Teotihuacán's ancestral funerary practices reached beyond its large city-state. Teotihuacán's practices of leaving a large amount of green obsidian artifacts at the ancestor's grave and the cylindrical form of the grave placed on its central axis have been found at the Copán burials of V-6 and XXXVII-8.[3] Copan's Temple of the Hieroglyphic Stairway was also elaborately decorated with Teotihuacán symbols, which along with the summit temple and tomb, comprised a conjoined ancestral shrine to the dead ruler, K'ahk' Uti' K'awill (628–695 CE).[4]

The tombs of the Oaxaca Barrio of Teotihuacán were found to have been reopened, sometimes with red pigment that was also likely reapplied over the human remains. The red color symbolizes or is related to the reverence of their buried ancestors. The practice of placing red pigment over the remains of their ancestors was also a trend that was utilized by many of the Classic Maya elite and may have also been a way to signify and facilitate their rebirth.[5]

Royal Maya tombs were designed to include all that the ancestor would need to live comfortably in the afterlife and make the arduous journey into the Underworld.[6] At Temple XIII in Palenque, there is a sarcophagus with the remains of a forty-year-old female ancestor of the seventeenth century known as the Red Queen. Her body was accompanied by a stunning jadeite mosaic mask, with numerous precious green stones, including bracelets and a diadem. Powdered cinnabar, red mercury oxide, covered her remains, a common practice in elite burials at Palenque.[7] At the Margarita tomb of Copán lies the richest female ancestor who was copiously covered with red pigments, hematite, and cinnabar.[8] The ancestor of Burial 9 at the Maya site, El Zotz, was covered in one layer of specular hematite and then one layer of red cinnabar.[9] The fabulous riches left at these royal burials ensured their continuing prestige and distinction in the afterlife nonordinary realms, wherein the ancestor could continue to enjoy these things.

The elite dead were often buried with beautiful polychrome ceramics, funerary furniture, stone ornaments, carved bone and shell, and elaborate jade jewelry, along with many other accoutrements. Pottery vessels were likely provided to ensure they had tableware to eat and drink from in the afterlife and possibly to release the energies of magical intentions within fermenting sealed vessels. Less wealthier ancestors were often buried with only a pot or two.[10] The size and shape of pottery vessels varied, as well as the types—bowls, drinking cups, and spouted vessels, which were likely a status marker of the individual. The name of the owner of the vessels was also often indicated on them, along with scenes of their possible solar apotheosis.[11]

Shards of broken vessels are also commonly found at burial sites.[12] The unusual patterns of residue at the burials of The Temple of the Sun at El Zotz suggest that the jars originally contained some sort of expanding or off-gassing liquid—perhaps the fermented sap beverage known as *pulque*. The "stopper" of the vessel prevented the gasses of the fermenting beverage from escaping. Eventually, the trapped pressure likely caused the bottom to burst and shatter.[13] Interestingly, one of my Maya mentors, Don Fernando, taught me a likely related magical recipe that involved a petition wrapped around a cinnamon stick with fruit and rum inside a ceramic vessel with a tight lid. The petition was a piece of parchment paper that had an intention written on it. He advised that inside the vessel now contained the spirits of the magic, and I was not to open it. He said that this allowed the magic to ferment and all would come into alignment. I remember when I went to Actun Tunichil Muknal (the Cave of the Stone Sepulchre), and I saw the broken ceramic shards, I thought of this particular magical recipe my mentor taught me. I sensed intuitively that the magic drawn on and within these vessels had fermented and been released.

Ancestors were also interred or cremated with their clothes. Mexica rulers, for example, were dressed in fifteen different vestments, and their bodies were decked in jewels. A jade bead was attached to the lower lip to serve as a heart. Their face was concealed under a mask and they were attired in the insignia of the god of the temple in which their ashes were to be deposited. Some of the jewelry often included: gold *bezote,* nose rings, labrets, ear pendants, armbands, diadems, crowns, bracelets, and necklaces.[14] A large quantity of mantles, breechcloth, sandals, colorful feathers, cacao, precious stones, and feather fans were also items that were offered to these esteemed ancestors.[15] They were also provided with a generous portion of different foods.[16]

While the offerings made to non-elite ancestors were not as extensive, their best mantles, loincloths, shrouded art, blankets, ceramic vessels, paper, pulque, and fine stones were left at their funerary sites.[17] To ensure they would not starve, they were provided with gourds of hens, stewed meat, bread, corn, beans, chia, and other legumes.[18] When it was a wealthier ancestor, officials of burial services were called, who cut up pieces of a paper made of tree bark (*amatl*) and covered the body of the deceased with them. They then dressed the body of the deceased according to the circumstances of their death. If the deceased had been a soldier, they dressed him as Huitzilopochtli. In other cases, ancestors were burned with a resinous pinewood effigy fully dressed in their clothes.[19]

Ancestors were also offered their tools of their trade. For the wealthier ancestors, their bodies and sacred items of comfort and transformation were placed in the fire. Fire consumed, purified, and

Fig. 2.1 Shows a bundled ancestor likely being prepared for a cremation ceremony as well as the diverse offerings—food, jewels, clothing, mirrors, blankets, and ceramics—that would be included in this ceremony. Including these sacred items in the cremation ceremony ensured that these items would be received by the ancestor and ensure their comfort and well-being in the afterlife.
Courtesy of Ancient Americas at LACMA. Codex Magliabechiano plate 69r.

transformed the deceased ancestor and their sacred items and allowed them to take with them items that would help them and provide comfort in the afterlife. When they died, these items would be waiting for them. Ancestors used these offerings to fortify themselves and receive necessary instructions to complete the journey into the afterlife. Fire also served as a conduit of power and communication between the living and their ancestors. Offerings, gifts, tears, and prayers were immediately transmitted to the ancestor via fire.[20]

Bodies that were buried rather than cremated were placed in deep trenches, wherein the corpse was often placed on a low chair with the implements of their trade or position.[21] Ancestors that had been merchants were also provided with items of their trade, including jaguar and deer skins, jewels, blankets, precious stones, gold objects, ceramic vessels, and rich plumage.[22] The Codex Magliabechiano plate 68r shows the burial of a merchant with rich offerings, as if they would have to use their trade as merchants in the afterlife.[23] Ancestors who had served in the military were offered items such as chert lanceolate points and animal skins.[24] In an excavation of a mass burial in San Andrés Cholula, ancestors whose trade was likely weaving were buried next to their spindle whorls, sewing implements, and layered textiles.[25]

Some items provided comfort for a specific place in the afterlife. Blankets were necessary to protect them against the low temperatures of the Underworld realms.[26] A red puppy was also buried or cremated with the ancestor as it was believed that it helped them to cross the Chiconahuapan River and guide them on the trek of the Underworld.[27]

Fig. 2.2 Shows the diverse offerings—food, jewels, clothing, mirrors, blankets, and ceramics—made specifically to a merchant ancestor. These items not only ensured their comfort and well-being but also enabled them to continue their trade as merchants in the afterlife.
(See also color plate 1.)
Courtesy of Ancient Americas at LACMA. Codex Magliabechiano plate 68r.

They also placed a vessel of water near the ancestor's remains to satisfy their thirst and bits of amatl paper to navigate and traverse safely through the land of the dead.[28] They said that the water served them in the afterlife.[29]

Sacred Items That Procured the Journey, Continuation, Renewal, and Rebirth of the Ancestor's Soul Energies

There were also certain sacred items that were believed to facilitate the ancestor's continuation, renewal, and rebirth of soul energies. Jade's linkage to themes of centrality, rulership, breath, and soul energy made it a key component of Maya funerary rites.[30] Bartolomé de las Casas, sixteenth-century missionary and ethnohistorian, indicates that a precious stone, likely jade or jadeite for wealthier ancestors and another type of green stone for less affluent ancestors, was placed in the mouth of a dying ancestor to catch his soul on its departure from the body. The stone was first rubbed over their face upon their death. The stone was then curated, and it was esteemed and offered sacrifices as if it were the ancestor, just as the ash containing effigies of the ancestor were treated.[31]

Shells, green stones, and deity accoutrements—headbands, masks, waist celts, necklaces, armbands, bracelets, ear plugs, and ankle tinklers—were placed on the ancestor, whether buried or cremated. Along with marking their status in the afterlife, they also likely contained aspects of and helped to strengthen the soul energy of the ancestor for their afterlife journeys, and in the cases of royal ancestors, helped to facilitate their apotheosis. Pakal II and the Red Queen of Palenque, for example, were each buried with a greenstone-encrusted headband across their brows, as well as with large, mosaic greenstone masks over their faces, smaller greenstone jade mosaic masks, and stone celts at their waist. Headbands were donned by rulers in accession rituals.[32] When Maya rulers wore the Principal Bird Deity, Ux Yop Huun, atop their heads, they likened themselves to the World Tree as the axis mundi. The donning of these headbands on their royal ancestors likely marked their importance and facilitated their continued access into the living and nonordinary realms.[33] Both Atlantic and Pacific species of *Spondylus* shells have also been found in Maya burials as containers for precious objects, tinklers, belts, and were placed over the heads and bodies of the ancestor.[34]

Maya stelae (slabs of stone), which were placed in front of ceremonial centers and political buildings and were carved with hieroglyphic inscriptions accompanying historical portraits to reflect the rise of a new political ideology and dynastic kingship, were sometimes interred with royal ancestors. These stelae also functioned as avatars that would hold a part of the depicted ancestor ruler's soul energy.[35] At Tikal, Stela 31 was buried in Temple 33. Continued offerings and fire ceremonies there suggest that they were most likely directed to ruler Sihyaj Chan K'awiil, who was present and embodied in Stela 31, and his corporeal remains, both of which were buried in the temple.[36] Stelae were also deliberately desecrated in war, claiming an aspect of the soul energy of the losing ancestor ruler and their city-state.[37] The burning of tombs likely operated to renew the soul energy of the mortuary space itself and perhaps even facilitated the solar accession and rebirth of the ruler.[38]

The sixteenth-century ethnohistorians that wrote about Central Mexican Indigenous practices indicated that a green stone, a *chalchíhuitl,* was placed in the mouth of the ancestor, which served as their heart in the afterlife, the teyolía soul energy. If they were less affluent, they used only greenish stones or obsidian. The deceased were believed to undergo a long and dangerous journey in the Underworld, which included different tests and trials. One of them involved having a ferocious jaguar ready to eat their heart. But this could be averted by placing a jade bead in the deceased's mouth at the funeral, which could then be offered to the jaguar in place of the heart.[39]

Fray Jerónimo de Mendieta, sixteenth-century ethnohistorian, also indicates that many of the items that provided comfort to the ancestor in their afterlife also helped the soul energy as teyolía to reach its destination.[40] They also buried ancestors with Colima duck effigies, which may have acted as spiritual guardians with implications of fertility and rebirth.[41]

Connect with the Ancestors:
Special Altars and Miniature Shrines

The altars created at funerary sites and the sacred ofrendas, such as censers, autosacrifice instruments, mirrors, and lintels, were multifaceted in purpose, in that they acted as portals for the ancestor to enter into the realms of the living, acted as sustenance for the ancestors, and invoked their presence, aid, and intervention. At Teotihuacán, ancestral altars were placed near the burials located within domestic central patios to honor their ancestors and keep them close to their homes and families.[42]

Altars or table shrines were often placed near royal and domestic Maya graves. In domestic settings they were near or above community patios or homes.[43] Little stone houses, lineage altars, were found near residential groups at Copán.[44] For the highland Postclassic Maya K'iché' lineages, these altars were known as *warabal ja,* sleeping houses for the ancestors.[45] These altars were likely places where the ancestors were conjured with offerings to ensure the ancestors' continued connection to the living.

For the Postclassic Yucatec Maya, ancestral miniature shrines are diminutive structures less than two meters square in each dimension, too small to accommodate a person of even the most modest stature. Most commonly, these buildings were one-room constructions that feature single entrances, made of masonry and mortar covered with a thick layer of limestone stucco plaster. They commonly had multiple stone altars set in front of and off the sides of shrine entrances and arranged at the base of stairways.[46] They were spaces where ancestors were honored and invoked.

Censers were also commonly found at funerary sites. The burning of offerings was one of the primary vehicles for awakening, feeding, summoning, communicating with, and renewing the soul energy of these burial sites, and transmitting the offering to their ancestor.[47] The elaborate censers of Teotihuacán depict a funerary cult centered on the butterfly soul that is released by cremation. The Ciudadela, the symbolic center of the Teotihuacán world, contains the largest known composite of ceramic censers, where approximately twenty thousand fragments and complete examples lie in the northwest portion of the Ciudadela.[48] An abundance of censers has also been recovered at Palenque, including on the lid of the Red Queen's sarcophagus when the tomb was opened.[49] Elaborate censers throughout ancient Mesoamerica include beautifully crafted ceramic pieces of ancestor portraits and ancestors conflated as deities, possibly signaling their deification.

Instruments of autosacrifice were also common items found at elite or royal ancestral funerary sites. Bloodletting, ingesting tobacco, drinking *balche* (an intoxicating beverage), and the burning of copal and petitions were ways to communicate with and invoke their ancestors.[50] The Maya elite drew blood from various parts of their bodies using lancets made of stingray spine, flint, bone, rope, or obsidian. The Yaxchilan Lintel 24 depicts Lady K'abal-Xok, the wife of the ruler Shield Jaguar II, engaging in autosacrifice with a thorn rope through her tongue, wherein the soul-animating energy of her blood facilitates a ritual communication with the living and the ancestors, a highly ritualized form of ancestral veneration.[51] Lintel 25 depicts them communing with the ancestor of their lineage, who is coming out of an anthropomorphic centipede serpent. Serpents, centipedes, and bearded dragons were often depicted as conduits for conjuring ancestors and other supernatural beings.[52] On the east side of Stela C at Copán, the Serpent Bar that ruler carries has ancestral beings coming out of it, wearing ornate stacked headdresses.[53] Stingray spines were also a common motif in Classic Maya art. Actual stingray spines and replicas in jade and other materials were found in tombs and were often placed in the pelvic area of men.[54]

Adult conch shells were used as trumpets in various kinds of ceremonies and were often incised with the name of the user or the ancestor being called forth. The Maya used them to communicate with supernatural beings and ancestors during bloodletting rites.[55] *Spondylus* mollusks were also provided at funerary sites, likely as a means for ritual ancestral communication and connection to the primordial waters of the Underworld.[56] Maya rulers were often portrayed with *Spondylus* necklaces, likely demonstrating their abilities to access the nonordinary realms of their ancestors and other supernatural beings.[57]

Mirrors of polished pyrite, hematite, or obsidian were also placed before or near ancestors and acted as portals for communing with ancestors.[58] At Burial 5 at Piedras Negras, the sacred items found at the funerary site included a hematite mirror that was found set at an angle, positioned to reflect the ruler's image.[59] Snakes often appear at the corners of mirrors depicting the arrival of ancestors from the afterlife.[60] At the Inner Murals of Chichen Itza, Register E depicts ancestor cartouches both as mirrors and as the Sun, with their ancestors emerging from the center of the sun-mirrors.[61]

The sensational artwork found at royal and elite funerary temples also provided private and public spaces for the living to commune with their ancestors. Some carvings, such as ones on the backs of monuments or the ones on the tops of tall monuments, regularly inaccessible to the living, were made for their ancestors to come to the realm of the living and admire.[62]

The breathtaking carvings within Pakal's tomb manifested ancestral veneration and the rebirth and apotheosis of the ancestor ruler's soul energy. The walls of the tomb of Pakal are decorated with nine large human figures that are holding a serpent staff topped by the head of K'awiil, a powerful and complex deity associated with lightning, ancestry, and fecundity.[63] These human figures are Pakal's ancestors, named by their headdresses, as seen on the side images of the sarcophagus.[64] A second series of ancestors, the very same as those formed in stucco on the walls, were carved onto the sarcophagus sides, depicted as ancestors emerging as fruit trees.[65]

The artwork at these funerary sites further facilitated ritually charged environments that enabled the living and ancestors to commune. The consecrated item the devotee may carry or place at the ancestor's altar served as a way for them to build upon their reciprocal performances and cross into each other's worlds. These devotional performances may include gazing into the carved image of their ancestors. Evoking the ancestors through devotional gazing and possibly other offerings was likely believed to lead to a "mutual gazing," wherein the ancestor became fully embodied in the image, and the living and ancestor were able to truly see and behold one another—a hierophany in action.

The layout of the funerary shrine and lintels of Tikal ruler, Jasaw Chan K'awiil, amplified and activated the visual trope of his conjuring.[66] In her illuminating analysis of Tikal's Temple I, Mesoamerican scholar Elizabeth Drake Olton proposes that this funerary shrine was a dynamic structure that housed a deceased ruler and, through its spatial environment, engaged the living. It was a transformative space that enveloped a visitor in an ensemble of experiences. The shrine can be separated into three main areas, possibly mirroring the tripartite nonordinary realms. The celestial shrine functioned as a sanctified location of mortuary ritual and transformation, connecting the living with the Upperworld nonordinary realms. It was designed to be both public and private. Those who walked the central corridor and moved through the rooms conceptually reentered the mortuary chamber of Jasaw, who commissioned this stunning funerary shrine.[67]

The massive funerary shrine, with its spacious Doorways 2 and 3, engaged participants through the emotional impact of the viewing experience of Lintels 2 and 3, which have double portraits of the former ruler. Lintel 2 is above the second doorway, wherein Jasaw faces West, the symbolic direction of death. His gaze would have met that of the communicant entering his shrine, guiding them toward the written text denoting his name. He is decked in Teotihuacán garb, but has several features associated with Maya ruler imagery—jaguar pelts, rounded shield, and jaguar skins.[68]

Lintel 3 spanned Doorway 3 and was above Burial 6, the most private and secluded of the shrine, possibly accessing the Underworld. He is depicted as a Classic-period Maya ruler, with a great, beaded-jade collar and three-piece pectoral. He is seated upon a mat, a way to denote the act of acceding to the throne, possibly an emergence or rebirth of a celestial accession.[69] The spatial composition and environment of Temple I draw the communicant as a ritual actor, an active ritual viewer who through this gazing evokes the ancestor and brings them into communion with one another.[70]

INTEGRATING ANCIENT MESOAMERICAN WISDOM
Creating Ancestral Altars

When we create a physical space for our ancestors to reside in and traverse, the connection and bond with our ancestors tends to greatly increase. We will draw from the wise ancient Mesoamericans to create altars that contain offerings that are multifaceted in purpose to strengthen our connections with them, provide love and comfort to them in the afterlife, and care for their soul energies. The ancestral altar can be for one or many ancestors. These stationary altars may contain items that can be mobile, but the altar itself is stationary and typically long-term. In chapter three, we will discuss temporary ancestral altars created for the three-day holiday, El día de los Muertos. In chapter five, we will delve into ancestral bundles that can be mobile and can be part of an altar. These bundles are a precious cloth or hide that charge and get charged by the sacred items we may carry in them.

Location of an Ancestral Altar

Once you have made your initial connection(s) with your ancestor (see pages 40–48), tune into their energy to find an ideal space for the ancestral altar in your home. Please consider asking yourself some of these initial questions in deciding where you should place your altar:

- What kind of connection do you share with them?
- How do you feel after connecting with them?
- Do you feel calm, centered, motivated, or healed by them?
- Is there a vocation, trade, or hobby you may you share with them?
- Do you perceive a closer connection to sacred land, space, family, or cultural roots when you connect with them?

Then, consider tuning into the unique energy of every room in your house through a physical walk-through or a mental intuitive scan, and ask your ancestor in which room and where within that room they would like their altar to be. I had a client who was in the process of creating a Mexican vegan menu for their business. One of the ancestors she had a deep connection with, her grandmother, was known for her delicious recipes. My client set up two altars: a small altar in the kitchen with items she would use for her cooking, which she knew were being blessed by her grandmother, and also one in her bedroom, so her grandmother could continue to inspire her with unique and flavorful Mexican vegan recipes while she slept.

Once you have decided which room and space to use for your ancestral altar, please also consider taking a moment to tune into the potential need to remove items that may not be a good fit for your ancestral altar. The space, furniture, and items that are presently there should feel like an energetic match with your ancestors—hopefully one that has a good energetic vibration. Creating an altar in a physical space that feels energetically aligned with your ancestors will ensure that you can also help your ancestors strengthen their soul-animating energies. This will also strengthen their abilities to intervene on your behalf, and effectively guide and aid you.

Stationary ancestral altars ideally should be created in peaceful physical spaces and can be any size. One time I had a client ask me if creating an ancestral altar at their workspace was acceptable. Before this, I had guided her to create an ancestral altar in her bedroom. She loved it and shared with me that it gave her an immediate sense of peace when she walked into her house, especially her bedroom. She wanted to infuse peace in her workspace with the help and intervention of her ancestor. While she had a nice office where she could close the door, if needed, her workspace overall was chaotic.

I recommended that she alternate between two to three sacred items from her ancestral altar and bring them to work with her, and then take them home at the end of the week to get cleansed and charged. This way the essence of the ancestor could be physically present with her in the office. This greatly helped with her anxiety and headaches at work. Needless to say, ancestral altars should be a place of rest and peace for our ancestors.

While ancestral altars can be any size, they should have a solid construction, as they can be sites of strong energy occurrences. Depending on the work you are doing with your ancestor, they may shake slightly because of the energy traveling through. Older wooden tables, chests, or the platform in general give off a feeling of antiquity, age, and wisdom. Yes, they definitely can make for a beautiful ancestral space. Just make sure these older pieces of furniture have a solid foundation.

Initial Cleansing and Cleaning

Before setting up the altar, it is highly recommended to clean and cleanse your ceremonial space. If your physical space is a disorderly mess, the energy of this physical reality will quickly trump the work to cleanse the space energetically. It is important to tidy up and do basic cleaning. I recommend including homemade (see pages 119–22) or store-purchased Florida water, or concentrated teas of lemon or orange blossoms, lemongrass, peppermint, and rosemary in your cleaning solutions to clean and cleanse the space or room for your ancestral altar. Please adjust as needed for a 32 fl. oz. cleaner:

- Boil ¼ cup of tea with a handful of any of the herbs or blossoms.
- Let it steep and cool for 8 minutes.
- While waiting for the tea to cool, fill a spray bottle about ⅔ full with your favorite cleaning solution.
- Add the cooled tea to your cleaning solution and mix well. Alternatively, you can fill the remainder of your cleaning solution with Florida water.

Along with basic cleaning, raise the vibration and lightness of the living space. Here are some other things you can do:

- Move furniture: Fix or get rid of broken furniture, make sure entries to rooms are clear and it is easy to walk around.
- Declutter: Gift unwanted belongings to friends and those in need, place stuff in appealing organizers, throw away garbage.
- Light: Make sure rooms get natural light during the day.
- Ancestral altar: Take everything off the space you are going to place

on your altar and clean it with your specially prepared cleaning solution.

After you have cleaned the space for your altar, cleanse it energetically with a space limpia. You can cleanse the room your ancestral altar is going to be in, or ideally, cleanse your whole house. If you are cleansing your whole house, open the main door to the house before you begin. If you are cleansing just a room of the house, you can open the windows of the room during or after the limpia.

You can give your space a limpia by lighting a bundle of herbs (such as sage, rosemary, cedar grass, or sweetgrass—all herbs have cleansing properties) and spreading the smoke from the herbs with a feather, feather fan, or your breath into every space of the room. You can also do a white fire limpia (see pages 38–39).

You may also consider placing any of the following sacred items to continuously absorb any dense energies in the room:

- Place any of the following crystals in a glass of water: obsidian arrowhead, green quartz, amethyst, citrine, and agate, and leave the glass by the door of the room. Dump out the water onto bare ground where nothing is growing and replace monthly.
- Fill a little less than half a glass with white rice and the other half with water. Leave the glass by the door of the room. Dump out the contents where nothing is growing and replace monthly or as needed.
- Plants are a wonderful way to naturally clear and recycle energies continuously. Here are some suggestions: succulents, cacti, roses, spider plants, and devil's ivy.

Cosmic Spacing

You may want to consider having your altar embody cosmic space, giving your ancestor and you access to traverse the nonordinary realms and obtain the gifts from these spaces. Many of us still divide our sacred spaces spatially or metaphorically through sacred items to embody a tripartite form, which was a vertical division of the nonordinary realms—Underworld, Middleworld, and Upperworld. (Refer to chapter one for the sacred gifts of the nonordinary realms: Upperworld: pages 30–33, Middleworld: pages 33–35, and Underworld: pages 35–37.)

The quadripartite realms can be expressed spatially or be metaphorical representations of the cardinal spaces and their cosmic soul energy gifts: South, discovery and understanding; West, death, release, and transformation; North, ancestral guidance, wisdom and medicine; East new beginnings and rebirth; and the Center as the axis mundi.

We can organize our altar spatially so the top of the altar is the Upperworld, the middle of the altar is the Middleworld with the cardinal spaces, and the bottom of the altar is the Underworld. Please keep in mind that while these spaces had their own wisdom and energy, oftentimes what they embodied could and did intersect and conflate with one another, so let yourself work intuitively in this cosmic representation. Here are ideas of sacred items that could be representations of these spaces on your altars:

SACRED TRIPARTITE ITEMS

REALM	ITEMS
Upperworld	favorite flowers, items that remind you of celestial or angelic beings, pictures of your ancestors, feathers of diurnal birds
Middleworld	earth, corn, favorite herbs, favorite crystals
Underworld	black crystals, geodes, feathers or other items from nocturnal animals

SACRED QUADRIPARTITE ITEMS

CARDINAL DIRECTION	MAYA COLOR	MEXICA COLOR	PURPOSE	SACRED ITEMS
South	yellow	blue	discovery	divination tools, tarot cards, sortilege, corn, shells
West	black	white	release	ayahuasca vines, peyote cacti, obsidian blades, *cascara sagrada*, dandelion root, burdock root, senna

CARDINAL DIRECTION	MAYA COLOR	MEXICA COLOR	PURPOSE	SACRED ITEMS
North	white	black	wisdom age	pictures of our elders, ancestors, fossils, shells, tree bark
East	red	red	rebirth renewal	water, jade, green stones
Center	blue	turquoise	connection history family	picture of ourselves or ancestors, sacred items that represent us or our ancestors

Sacred Items for the Altar

Inspired by the wise ancient Mesoamericans, who loved and were devout in their ancestral veneration practices, please consider placing sacred items that have multifaceted purposes and roles. While I provide examples of items that can do so in this next section, most importantly the items have to resonate with you, so they have meaning and impact. Such items will invoke the ancestors' presence, aid, and intervention; provide them comfort in the afterlife; strengthen their soul energies; and act as portals from and into the nonordinary realms of the afterlife.

Keep in heart and mind that all items that are placed on the ancestral altar will be infused with the soul energies of your ancestors. Before placing anything on your ancestral altar, please consider cleansing it by placing the item carefully over: the orange flames of a white fire limpia (see pages 38–39), smoke from a charcoal tablet and copal (aka *sahumerio*), or a lit herbal smudge bundle. Alternatively, spray it with your homemade Florida water (see pages 119–22) or buy Florida water from a store, or find another way you feel the item wants to be cleansed. After cleansing it, hold the item to your heart and thank your ancestor or ancestors for blessing and infusing their soul energies into the sacred item, and of course, this infusion and blessing can be a ceremony in and of itself. As discussed in chapter one, it is not required to place an actual image of an ancestor on the ancestral altar. Rather it can be a picture or an item that literally or metaphorically represents them.

These items may be any of the following:

- A picture of a sacred land. If you feel connected to the ancestors of a sacred site or land, a picture of the land can strengthen the link between you and your ancestors.
- A fresh or dry medicinal plant. If you have an inherent green thumb or intuitive knowledge about plants and their gifts, and you sense that your plant affinity is associated with an ancestor or ancestors, the plant will help breathe life into your ancestral connection.
- A religious or sacred item. Ancestors who were devotees of a faith (including nonmonotheistic faiths) or believed in some kind of divine power will be drawn to sacred items. These items can also continue to strengthen their soul-animating energies in the afterlife.
- Tools of a trade. If your ancestors had a trade they loved, place something that is a part of or represents this trade. Your ancestors can use these tools in the afterlife and will be drawn to them at the altar.
- Tools of a hobby or craft. If your ancestors had a hobby or craft they loved to engage in, place something that is a part of or represents this hobby to strengthen your connection and welcome them to the altar.
- Items they actually wore or you feel they would love, such as clothing, jewelry, blankets, *rebozos* (shawls), or accessories can provide our ancestors comfort in the afterlife and invite their presence on our altar.
- Power items, such as crystals, staffs, rattles, drums, figurines, ancestral bundles, popoxcomitl, censers, and ladles that are specifically for your ancestral altar are also power items that can be transported to different places and invite your ancestors to have greater access to you in these spaces.
- Books about a shared culture or about them can create or strengthen the connection between you and your ancestors.

Sor Juana Inez de la Cruz, seventeenth century feminist, prolific philosopher and composer, for example, continued to come forward for me as a cultural ancestor. When I felt a strong intuitive pull to invite her as part of my ancestral entourage, I placed a book of her life on my altar and humbly invited her as such.

- Figurines. Creating figurines that represent our ancestors is an ongoing tradition. Consider for the next Day of the Dead celebration making *calaveras* (skulls) of your ancestors as a ceremonial crafting celebration (see pages 87–88).

Portals: Tools of Travel

There are also sacred items that are still understood to act as sacred portals from and into the nonordinary realms. Some of these sacred items include:

- Water: Consider placing a cup of water on your altar and using it as an ofrenda and a portal to send messages, prayers, and love to your ancestors.
- Mirrors: Place a regular mirror or traditional polished pyrite, hematite, and obsidian mirror on your ancestral altar to access your ancestors and provide your ancestors access to their altar.
- Fire: The wick of a candle can act as a portal for our ancestors. Gazing into the wick of the candle with deep intentional inhales and exhales is also a way for us to commune with and invoke our ancestors.

Sustenance: Food, Drink, Aroma, and Vessels

Aromas, especially pleasant aromas, are something our ancestors consume and are composed of. Copal is a sacred resin from a tree that is indigenous to the Americas that we still use to cleanse our spaces, recognize them as sacred, and to attract divine aid, including and especially our ancestors. I also like to leave the bottle tops of my oils open for them at least once a month as an offering. Oil diffusers also serve as wonderful aromatic offerings for our ancestors.

Aromatic food or drinks are also traditional in feeding and sustaining the soul energy of our ancestors. The sweet intoxicating smell of fresh pastries is believed to traverse the nonordinary realms. Since I make it a practice to recycle offered food into the earth, I opt to share compostable friendly food with my ancestors.

Ideal beverages are ones we feel our ancestors will enjoy or that we enjoy the most. Personally, I serve them my first beverage of choice, delicious refreshing water. Aside from kombucha and occasional coconut water, water is what I typically drink, and I feel that my ancestors who I connect with the most are also water lovers like me. When I host cacao ceremonies and make cacao beverages for myself, my ancestors are the first to get served.

Another traditional custom for our ancestors is to set aside specific cups and plates for them.

Cleansing

It is ideal to cleanse the altar(s) cyclically, which can be once a week, each month, every six months, or once a year; you define the cycle. The cleanses can include:

- making offerings of copal
- spraying the altar with cleansing waters, such as Florida water, rose water, or lavender water
- frequencies and sound, such as drums, songs, poems, spoken word, Tibetan bowls, crystal bowls
- smudging with bundles of herbs
- white fire limpias (refer to pages 38–39)
- taking everything off the altar and cleansing the foundation and the items with your specially prepared cleaning solution, or soap and water

If you feel a nudge to cleanse the altar, take a moment to connect with your altar and ask your altar about its changes, so you can make time to do so. Let yourself be intuitively guided as to whether a new layout is needed or whether items need to be moved elsewhere or other items should be included.

As for potentially portable sacred items that are on our ancestral altars, like pictures, talismans, instruments, or crystals, it is wonderful to bring them with us to classes, ceremonies, work, or just to have them on us. Make sure they come back to get recharged periodically. Ask them when they are ready to come back home to their altar to get recharged. Please also consider smudging each item with a bundle of dry herbs, cleansing them with copal, spraying them with Florida water, or if they fit, placing them inside a crystal or Tibetan bowl and playing the bowl while they are inside of it to cleanse them before placing them back on the altar.

DYNAMICS OF ELIZABETH'S OFFICE SHIFTS

When Elizabeth first came to me, she was experiencing what she felt were unusual bouts of anxiety at work and headaches. She worked at a bank handling what she claimed were the less glamorous aspects of accounting, compliance. She was good at her job and felt relatively satisfied with it. There was a newer team, however, she had been overseeing for the last eight months that was incredibly difficult, disrespectful to her, and on more than one occasion attempted to blame her for their mistakes. She identified them as the "problem team." She oversaw two other teams, whom she loved. Unfortunately, she had to spend more time with the problem team because there were issues that came up in the problem team's audit the prior year.

Elizabeth was an absolute sweetheart. She was still recovering from a heartbreak but was upset with herself for still feeling sad about the heartbreak. Her boyfriend, with whom she had lived and dated for six years, somewhat unexpectedly left her. During our first session, I was guided to ask her about her love life. She responded immediately that it was fine, and then retracted with, "Well, it is not existent." She admitted to me off the bat that she was upset with herself for still being hurt by someone who left her, something that happened more than two years prior. Her father passed away when she was eight, her mother had recently passed away, her grandparents had already passed, and most of her family were in Mexico and Nicaragua. Apparently, when her boyfriend left her, her job gave her a promotion and raise. It provided something she could be proud of and kept her heart and mind occupied, at least initially, after the breakup. Shortly after her mother passed away, Elizabeth inherited the problem team.

Immediately after our first session, I sensed that Elizabeth's headaches and anxiety were also connected with her feelings of being alone and somewhat rootless, without family and ancestors. She also admitted to me that she had never met her family from Nicaragua and had met some of her family from Mexico on a few occasions during her childhood and teenage years. I felt two great-great-grandmother ancestors come up for her during our session, one from Mexico and another one from Nicaragua. I knew these ancestors were ready to help Elizabeth with the problem team and to help remind her that she is always rooted in ancestral love.

I encouraged her to create a cultural ancestral altar at her home. I asked her what made her happy when she thought about Mexico and Nicaragua. She laughed and told me plantains for Nicaragua and enchiladas for Mexico. I said that was beautiful, and something connected with the food she loves from these places needed to be on her altar. I also encouraged her to go on the internet, explore beautiful places within these countries, places she would consider visiting. I recommended she include pictures of these places, items for cooking her favorite foods from these places, and pictures and mementos of her mother and father. I recommended that she invite her father and then mother for a cup of coffee and share with them whatever else she was having for breakfast, when she could make time to do so in the mornings. In these conversations, she could let them know what had been going in her life and begin sharing with them anything left unsaid.

In our next session, she told me that although it was very difficult to connect with her parents, after a few exchanges with them she began to feel a lightness in her heart. She was able to do this at least a couple times a week, since she was working principally from home and went into work one to two days a week because of the pandemic. She shared with me that along with the items I recommended, she included a rosary, images of Our Lady of Guadalupe, and a large, beautiful jasper crystal heart on her ancestral altar. The rosary and Our Lady of Guadalupe helped her feel connected to her mother and the women in her family, as many women, including her mother, were devout Catholics. The jasper symbolized her heart becoming whole after losing her father at such a young age. At our next session, I suggested that in her following breakfast conversations with her mother and father, she could relay to them what was transpiring at work and bring the rosary for her mother and jasper heart for her father, depending on who she was speaking with. I also recommended bringing those sacred ancestral items to work when she went into work or to have them by her laptop when she was working from home.

In our next session, she shared with me that after two weeks of bringing the rosary and the jasper crystal heart with her to work, the principal instigator of the bad team had been relocated to another division. She told me the bad team seemed to be more responsive and less confrontational. They were still, however, very different than the other two teams she managed. Her anxiety and headaches were almost nonexistent. Due to the pandemic, there were also talks of internal restructuring. This possible restructuring meant that she would no longer be overseeing the bad team and instead would pick up another team and office that was closer to her home. Elizabeth was elated and asked if she could create an ancestral altar at work. I encouraged her to keep her ancestral altars in a place they could rest and be at peace, ideally her home. I recommended she engage in a reciprocal performance of devotion.

Since food was an immediate and instinctual connection for Elizabeth with her ancestors, I recommended that for one year, she rotate a monthly feast for her mother and her ancestors from her mother's line, and then the next month for her father and her ancestors from her father's line and in exchange, that they help her to create an ideal work environment and circumstances. I told her to write her request and her devotional offering on a petition and leave it on the altar. Elizabeth's eyes were sparkling like I had never seen before. She was definitely excited.

By Elizabeth's next session, she had just finished her second devotional feast. She came in with great news. By the next month, she would no longer be managing the problem team and would be managing three teams that were all close to where she lived—two of which were teams that she had already been managing and got along with very well. Her anxiety and headaches were gone, and any residuals were being managed with the shamanic breathwork I had taught her. The following month, I received a text from her informing me that her new team was very pleasant and she enjoyed working with them thus far.

Elizabeth has continued her monthly devotional feasts to her ancestors. Through these devotional performances and offerings, she admitted that she felt closer to her ancestors, more than ever before, and finally felt strong enough to work on and heal her prior romantic heartbreak. Opening to her ancestors has given Elizabeth the courage and strength to go deeper on her path of healing and claim her happiness on every level of her life.

CHAPTER 3

Colorful Ceremonies Honoring Our Ancestors

Regular and spontaneous ceremonies for our ancestors, in which we shower them with gratitude and love, strengthen their soul energies and our connection to one another. Along with my regular ofrendas to my ancestors, I also hold annual and spontaneous celebrations for my ancestors, which typically include limpia rites, art, crafts, costuming, altar-making, music, sound baths, cacao ceremonies, and whatever else I am guided to engage in. As for regular ceremonies, for El día de los muertos, every year my husband, Miguel Buenaflor, and I engage in some kind of private or community ritual ancestral craft-making that will house our ancestors and be placed somewhere in our house or will sit on our ancestral altar.

We may also celebrate the month of Xocotl Uetzi (per the Gregorian calendar, likely August 1st through August 20th), the month ancestors were believed to return and our Central Mexican ancestors celebrated their ancestors. We hold online and in-person lunar sound bath ceremonies, wherein we teach, recognize, and honor our sacred traditions, encourage others to connect with their ancestors in our guided sound journeys, and include a few items from my ancestral altar to join us in this celebration. The spontaneous and private ceremonies vary in style, and I allow myself to work intuitively as to when I am being called to celebrate my ancestors. Sometimes they involve creating sacred space by placing copal on a charcoal tablet and singing a song I wrote for them, or on a full or new moon I will make cacao for myself and my ancestors and invite them to sing and dance with me.

The reclaiming of my ancestors, my culture, and myself have definitely coincided with my own bumpy, exciting, and dynamic processes of healing. For a good portion of my childhood and adolescence, the man my mother remarried, who was also Mexican, demanded assimilation from my mother and me in very nasty ways. He chastised my mother for her Spanish accent, repeatedly told me that my last name made me sound like a wetback, discouraged us from speaking Spanish in our home, and told me that if I was fortunate, I would not look like my father, who looked like an "Indio" ("Indigenous").

It was bad enough growing up in the eighties, where assimilation was expected by the status quo and most institutions, but being bombarded by this at home was incredibly traumatizing. It was not until I got to college in my Xicanx courses that I was finally provided with the tools to begin to deconstruct, decolonize, and heal my mind, heart, and soul. In these processes of decolonization came the celebration and reclamation of my ancestors in public and private ceremonies. Although it was never my initial intent, over the years I have definitely noticed small and large "miracles" of my ancestors intervening more readily on my behalf. Working with clients and inspiring them to reclaim and decolonize themselves and their ancestors, I have also noticed their ancestors intervene on their behalf, especially in light of their devotional daily rituals, regular ancestral celebrations, and spontaneous ones. These devotional ancestral ceremonies are so incredibly helpful to heal, reclaim, and decolonize ourselves and, of course, strengthen our connection to our ancestors and our ancestors' soul energies, giving them greater access to intervene on our behalf.

Similarly, ancient Mesoamerican peoples engaged in numerous state, calendrical, community, familial, and individual rites to honor their ancestors and keep them as active players in their lives. In these rites, their ancestor's presence came forward in diverse ways. These rites enabled and secured, among many things, their ancestor's obligation and ability to intervene, aid, legitimize, and guide their living patrons, and strengthened their connections and access to one another. These ceremonies involved ritual dancing, creating sacred spaces for ritualized offerings, reentry of funerary sites to make offerings, and manipulation of their ancestor's bones—resilient seeds for rebirth of the ancestor's soul energy, sacred tools used for conjuring and communicating with their ancestors and for ancestral deification.[1] The rites also involved ritual performances—dancing, weeping, and singing and cyclical ceremonies after their ancestor's death.

Along with regular private domestic rites for their ancestors, there were also annual calendrical ceremonies that honored the memory of their ancestors in different ways. After delving into ancient Mesoamerican ancestral veneration rites, I will draw from this wisdom to then explore different kinds of ceremonies we can engage in to venerate our ancestors and strengthen our connections with one another, as well as strengthen our connections with our ancestors as a family, including teaching children about their ancestral roots and connections using creative and fun activities. I will also delve into a story of one of my clients who used veneration rights to clear an ancestral curse that was affecting both her and her daughters.

RITUAL PERFORMANCES: DANCING, MOURNING, SINGING, AND ABSTENTION

Ritual performances to venerate ancestors took on many dimensions. They included performances that would allow the performer to channel or retrieve messages from ancestors and embody the ancestor through costuming, consuming entheogens orally or via enemas, dancing, bloodletting, or gazing into fire, water, and sacred objects, such as pyrite or obsidian mirrors and staffs.[2] Various Classic Maya artwork depict ancestors moving into and from the world of the living and the Flowery Realm of ancestors and supernatural beings through mirrors, implying that mirrors acted as portals that allowed movement into and from the realms of the living and nonordinary realms.[3]

Ritualized trance dancing often involved Maya rulers, lords, and commoners dressed in masked costumes that represented the ancestors into whom they transformed or channeled as they performed.[4] The performers' trance state of consciousness in many of these ritual performances facilitated the journey of the deceased into the realms of the living. Mesoamerican scholar Stephen Houston notes that when the hieroglyphic frequency of when the soul of a living human "concurred," or joined with the soul of a deity or deified ancestor, the event was facilitated by movement, especially of the feet, likely dancing.[5]

The sacred accoutrements, objects, and instruments used in these ritual performances also served as portals or facilitated the journey of the ancestors into the realms of the living. Performers often wore costumes and accessories, such as canes and staffs, that were believed to attract the ancestor and allowed the performer to communicate with or embody them during the performance. Belts of representative ancestral heads were common royal dance regalia in Maya ritual ancestral dancing, and the Maya accessed their ancestors through dance.[6] Ocarinas and ceramic drum fragments from palatial quarters and ordinary residences likely provided musical accompaniment to these ritual ancestral performances.[7] Musical performances and other forms of entertainment at lavish banquets filled with offerings of foods and gifts in honor of and for the ancestors were also a frequent occurrence.[8]

There are also extensive ethnohistorical records that detail the elaborate Postclassic Central Mexican ritualized performances that were believed to facilitate the departure and subsequent journey of the ancestor into the nonordinary realms and were intended to ease the pain of their survivors. These performances were largely ones of mourning, veneration, and abstention.[9] Songs and chants that praised the deeds of the ancestor were sung at their funeral.[10] The music that was played at the funeral was special and different from the music that was played at other celebrations. The rites did not end with the burial of the body but lasted until the ancestor's soul energies had reached their destination.[11]

When husbands died, for example, after the singing and chanting by all funerary attendees, the widows, their sons and daughters, and all

Fig. 3.1 Palenque, Tablet Panel. Carved limestone depicting the dancing
ceremony in veneration of an ancestor. The central figure, K'inich K'an Joy
Chitam II, stands in a dancing posture. His father, K'inich Janaab Pakal (right),
and mother, Lady Tz'akbu Ajaw (left) sit flanking him. The text records an
anniversary of the death of his ancestor, K'an Joy Chitam I.

Courtesy of Ancient Americas at LACMA. SD-120.

Drawing by Linda Schele. Copyright © David Schele.

their relatives began their somber performances. All the women wore their hair loose, hanging close to their faces. The wives wore their husband's mantles and breechcloths draped over one shoulder, while their sons and daughters carried in their hands their feather ear ornaments, labrets, and all of their fathers' jewels.[12] They would dance and sing, wailing, screaming, clapping their hands to the beat of the instrument, bowing toward the earth, inclining their bodies, and raising their bodies continuously.[13] After they had danced quite a long time, they sat down to rest. The mourners were then supported by the community and offerings were given to them.[14]

The mourners also made mummy bundle statutes of their ancestors out of pine torch. They put together many strips of this resinous wood, tied them together with cords called *aztamecatl* (white rope) and adorned them with small banners and mantles, and placed them on the deceased's altar. The old men performers began to sing and dance the funeral chants and did so for four days. On the fourth day, they set fire to the pine torch bundles and buried the ashes.[15]

The old men performers, and all the relatives—men, women, and children—thereafter engaged in abstention ritual performances. They took part in a light fast for eighty days, wherein they ate one meal a day. Abstention is often premised on the understanding that ancestral guides that have crossed over do not rely on the many things humans rely on to survive. Hence, by forgoing in the enjoyment of what we typically rely on, abstention was likely believed to bring the living and ancestor closer together and strengthen their connection.

Another aspect of abstention involved not washing their faces or combing their hair. After the eighty days, the priests removed the crust of dirt that had accumulated on the cheeks of the mourners. They wrapped the filth in paper and took it to *Tzatzcantitlan* (place where wailing ends). Clothes and food were given to the old men performers for five days.[16] Every four years thereafter, for four days, they burned offerings of copal, food, pulque, and flowers, to aid and strengthen the ancestor's teyolía in the afterlife, and engaged in different abstention rituals, including light fasts. At the fourth year, the funeral services

Fig. 3.2 Depicts the funeral of a ruler as a bundle going into a
fiery pit of cremation, the offerings that were being included in the
cremation, and the Mexica's somber crying ceremonies. These wailing
ceremonies enabled the release of the ancestor's soul energies and
also were fundamental in the healing and release of the families.
(See also color plate 2.)
Courtesy of Ancient Americas at LACMA. Codex Magliabechiano, plate 67r.

were terminated.[17] Women were in charge of lunar mourning ceremonies, and the old men were in charge of the solar mourning, wherein the
old men informed the Sun of the ancestor's arrival.[18]

REENTRY RITUALS:
EXHUMATION AND BONE MANIPULATION

Ancestral veneration rituals, especially for elite ancestors, often
took place long after interment and included reentry of burials for

exhumation, bone manipulation, and various other ancestral rites. At a tomb in El Zotz, it was likely left open for weeks or more to allow protracted funerary rituals, long after the ruler was interred.[19] The reentry of funerary sites often involved the relocation, removal, or addition of ancestral bones and artifacts.[20]

Bones were believed to contain or be a seed of the ancestor's soul energy, were venerated in their own rites, and were often depicted with life-affirming symbols, such as flowers and jewels.[21] Certain bones were believed to contain certain powers and were used in ancestor and spirit conjuring.[22] The Classic-period Maya believed certain body parts, most notably the head, retained aspects of an individual's identity and likely their soul energy.[23] In ethnohistoric Maya cosmology, human bones held a particularly important association with corn. In the creation story of the *Popol Vuh,* an old woman, older than the gods, mixed water and finely ground corn powder to make human beings.[24]

During veneration reentry rites, ancestor bones may also have been subject of a burning veneration.[25] As I explain in *Cleansing Rites of Curanderismo,* fire limpia rites were used to renew and activate the soul energies of sacred buildings and spaces, including mortuary spaces.[26] The burning of bones may have also served to renew the soul energies of the ancestor. The burning and censing of Burial 13 at Classic Maya site Piedras Negras likely served to revivify the ruler's remains. The pattern of burning indicates that the bone was burned after the body had already skeletonized.[27]

Bone manipulation also included defleshing, cutting, drilling, and grinding of long bones and teeth, as well as the removal and intentional postmortem spatial manipulation of skeletal elements.[28] Dead body manipulations might have also been associated by the Maya with anniversaries of important calendrical ceremonies, as well as with anniversaries of the death of the ancestor.[29] These manipulated bones were often placed in bundles and were often venerated as the ancestor themselves.[30]

Ancestor skulls for the Postclassic Maya were particularly revered as the ancestor themselves and were kept in the oratories of houses, next to their ancestral statues and ashes. Small family oratories or altars served as ritual loci for ancestral veneration. They placed a kind of bitumen over the skull to give it a living appearance of the ancestor and paid it great respect and reverence. On all of their festival days, they made offerings of food to the ancestor.[31] The skull seemed to represent or memorialize the ancestor in life.[32]

For the Central Mexicans, the vital soul energy force resided in the bones.[33] The Mexica sometimes removed the femur from a body after death because of its religious symbolism. Femurs stood for continuity and fertility and were sometimes hung from a tree for display outside the house. Femurs were also cut with deep parallel grooves to make a kind of rasp or musical instrument for ceremonies. Grooved femurs were very common in the western part of the Aztec Empire, often reburied with offerings as secondary burials.[34]*

Ancestral bones were also blessed and anointed with blue pigments. Fernando de Alvarado Tezozómoc, a sixteenth-century ethnohistorian, indicates that during the funeral of Tízoc, both his corpse and remains after cremation were doused with "blue water." The so-called "blue water" could owe its color to the presence of a pigment. If this liquid was sprayed on the incandescent remains, it would cause, by the sharp change in temperature, increased fragmentation. As the water evaporates, by the heat of a recently extinguished pyre or with the passage of time, the pigment attached to the bone.[35]

SOLAR CALENDRICAL RITES

The ethnohistorical records concerning the annual calendrical feast celebrations indicate that the Postclassic Central Mexicans engaged in numerous other ceremonies to honor their ancestors. It was believed

---

*A "primary" burial contains the skeletal material of one or more individuals, but the remains have not been manipulated after death or before burial. A "secondary" burial is one in which the skeleton has been disarticulated or moved.

that the veils of reality were incredibly thin certain days of the year, and ancestors were able to traverse the realms of the living. Celebrations and feasts were held to honor their ancestors and entice them to join the celebration and festivities.

For the month of Toxcatl, they celebrated feasts for their deities, Titlacauan, master builder, and Tezcatlipoca, smoking mirror, and engaged in many rituals in honor of these deities and what they facilitated. During their feast for likely Titlacauan, they also honored their ancestors and the figurines of their ancestors with offerings. The state celebration honoring their ancestors was held in the Huitzilopochtli Temple, while families throughout the Aztec empire honored their ancestors at home and within their communities.[36]

For the month of Tlaxochimaco in late summer, they celebrated the feast of *Micailhuitontli* (Little Feast of The Dead), wherein they made offerings of chocolate, candles, fruit, breads, native wine, and various other kinds of food and pine torches. There is some disagreement as to whether the celebrations in the month of Tlaxochimaco were done to commemorate deceased children, or whether it was a minor festival, a kind of preparation for the feast of *Hueymiccailhutl* (The Great Feast of the Dead).[37]

The Hueymiccailhutl was celebrated the following month, Xocotl Uetzi, wherein ancestors returned to Earth to celebrate with the living.[38] One of the celebrations included a race wherein men climbed a *xocotl* (pole), a tall tree at least one hundred ten to one hundred forty feet tall, and tried to get to the top to knock down a figurine made of *tzoalli* (amaranth seed) of Otontecuhtli, a god of death. The winner cut off the head of Otontecuhtli and was allowed to keep a piece of Otontecuhtli in their home for one solar year.[39] Similar to their other idols, this figurine had likely been activated with the sacred essence energy of Otontecuhtli, so keeping a piece of the figurine was a great honor. Otontecuhlti appeared as a warrior bundle adorned with paper butterflies, referring to the butterfly soul released during the burning of an ancestral bundle.[40]

For the month of Tepeilhuitl (Feast for the Mountains), they celebrated a feast in honor of the high mountains, where it was believed were places of origin. Many feasts and ceremonies were held within mountains. They made *ecatotonti* (idols) made of wood overlaid with dough to represent and embody an ancestor. They also made images in memory of those who drowned in the water. After many ceremonies, they placed the ecatotonti on their altars, offered tamales and other food, gave verbal praise, and drank wine in their honor.[41]

For the month of Quecholli, they honored Mixcoatl, one of their principal gods of hunt, and prepared many rites to ensure that animals would fall into the hands of the hunter. The festival also honored ancestors.[42] For four days they made numerous small arrows and bound them in fours with four pine torches. Along with the torches and arrows, they placed two tamales at the graves of their ancestors. They stayed at the graves all day. At night, they burned them and engaged in ritual dancing, singing, and fire ceremonies for their ancestors. At nightfall, ancestors and deities had greater access to the earthly planes and were fed by these performative offerings.[43]

INTEGRATING ANCIENT MESOAMERICAN WISDOM

Ancestral Veneration Ceremonies

The ceremonies that the ancient Mesoamericans engaged in to venerate their ancestors integrated rites that allowed the living and ancestors to traverse each other's realms. This was done through performances that procured a trance or meditative state and were performed on days and times of the day where the veils of reality were thinner. Along with breathwork and movement, engaging in ceremonial art projects that involve ancestral veneration—coupled with performing them on days and times of day, wherein the veils of reality are thinner—are ideal ways to not only strengthen our connection with our ancestors, but to also traverse each other's realms.

Ceremonial Art-Making for Ourselves and Family

Art is a wonderful way to quiet the mind and tune into gifts and messages from our ancestors, invoke and inspire their presence and aid, and provide them a home or space for them to join the living. The following are traditional ceremonial art projects that have their roots in ancient Mesoamerica and modern curanderismo traditions. While many of these are performed on particular days, such as birthdays or the three-day celebration of El día de los muertos, any day or time we feel the urge to honor and connect with our ancestors is the perfect day or time to engage in these ceremonial projects.

Art is also a wonderful way to bring families together, share stories about family members and larger cultural understandings, and teach children about their ancestral roots and connections with creative and fun activities. If my clients have children and I feel they may be open to it, I always recommend including their family and especially their children in these ritual craft-making activities to venerate our ancestors and strengthen our connection with them. My clients who have engaged in these activities with their children have shared that they often spark a deeper curiosity within them as to their cultural and familial heritage, as well as a sense of pride as to their own identities and familial and cultural relations. It is also usually fun and relaxing for the family.

We can also use ritual craft-making to heal our inner child and help them feel rooted to our familial and cultural ancestors. This is particularly helpful if you, like me, did not feel rooted to your ancestors or a part of any culture during your childhood. Personally, even though I was a dual citizen, Mexican and American, I never really felt Mexican, nor did I feel "American," and was cut off from my family and culture for a good portion of my childhood and teenage years. Moving to the States permanently made me a *gringa* (a somewhat derogatory term for a U.S. resident or citizen), no longer Mexican, and I experienced a good amount of racial discrimination to make me feel like an outsider in the States. Being in this in-between rootless dissociative space haunted me into my adult years. These ritual craft-making projects venerating my ancestors were critical in helping me to heal both my inner child and inner teenager, and help them-me feel connected to my family and culture.

Before engaging in ancestral veneration craft-making, I take a moment to invite my inner child and sometimes my inner teenager to join me; my inner child is typically the one who is most interested in these activities. I reflect on the beauty and grace to which I am connected through my ancestors and allow this to be expressed in these projects. I would have loved to engage in these projects as a child and to learn about and honor my deceased relatives as well as my culture. But it is never too late to give our inner child and inner teenager what they would have loved to experience and receive—in this case, feeling rooted by rich and beautiful ancestral traditions.

Calavera Making

Making candy or air-dry clay skulls is one of my personal favorite ways to honor and even connect with new ancestors. Molds for calaveras can be purchased, but I typically use my hands and my tools from my Play Doh sets or silverware to shape the teeth and eyes.

For this candy calavera recipe you will need the following:

- Preferably a 1.5-quart mixing bowl
- 2 egg whites
- 4 cups of white granulated or coconut sugar
- 10 tsp of water
- Colored icing tubes

Place the egg whites, water, and the sugar in the bowl. Whisk them together and squeeze the ingredients with your hands. Because the water will settle to the bottom, make sure you bring the water to the top, squeezing everything together, until the sugar feels like wet sand at the beach. If the sugar feels too dry, include two more teaspoons of water in the mix. Roll the mix into a round ball, then begin to make and shape your calavera head. Let it dry for twenty-four hours and decorate the skull with colored frosting. It is customary to include the name of the ancestor on the calavera, as well as accessories for the head, such as earrings, hats, moles, cigars, or nose rings.

Before placing the calavera on your ancestral altar, consider offering copal or incense to it and take a moment to connect with the calavera. Confirm that they indeed want to be placed on the altar and find out where on the altar they want to be placed. Thereafter, consider making the calavera offerings of libation, food, or sweets, helping to begin to enliven the calavera with the soul energy of your ancestor and help them feel welcomed on the altar. Check in periodically to see where it wants to be placed. If you made a candy calavera, tune in as to whether you should partake in eating the calavera after having it on your altar for at least a day or two. One of my mentors shared with me that we become closer with ancestors by doing so.

Calaca (Skeleton) Scenes

Calaca scenes may take more time to create and they are a wonderful way to connect with vocational and cultural ancestors. What is traditionally done is to create a scene that portrays that ancestor's skill, trade, vocation, or home, or a cultural space that contains items that help us feel connected to our ancestors.

I created a cultural calaca scene that helped me connect with my grandfather. It has bold burgundy wallpaper, a dining table with traditional clay Mexican plates, cups, and pastries, and my grandfather and friends he would entertain. My grandfather was incredibly charismatic and loved to entertain. I also have Frida's artwork on the walls. Although my grandparents did not have Frida's artwork in their home, I included items that made me feel connected to and love my Mexican culture and my grandfather.

Most craft stores have most if not all of the items you'll need for your calaca scene. These are some ideas:

- A little wooden rectangular or square box where the lid can be removed
- Air-dry clay to make the furniture and accessories to create your calaca scene
- Textured or colored paper for wallpaper

- Small calacas (find them many places online)
- Optional: small trinkets, dollhouse furniture, and tiny accessories

🎭 *Making a Calaca Scene*

Start this ceremonial craft-making by inviting your ancestors with copal, sharing a drink, and bringing an ancestral item from your altar to your workspace. Say a prayer and thank them for their inspiration and guidance. Before I start ceremonial art projects, I designate a preferred day for the next few months and commit to it. Because this is a ceremonial project, it is important to set aside time and space for it to ensure that our ancestors and roots are not forgotten about. Tune into the energy of the ancestor and ask them to join and guide your craft-making. This will be a sacred space for them to visit and reside in.

Once it is completed, tune in and see where it wants to go.

My calaca scene went in my living room, as my grandfather wanted to be a part of any entertaining we did and to be with us when we were celebrating holidays.

Decorating Frames

Many craft stores also sell inexpensive plain frames that we can paint and decorate with sweet trinkets, like a mortar and pestle, plates, cups, and rhinestones. Before engaging in decorating the frame, again, invite your ancestors and ask them who would like a picture frame, unless you know who it is for. Inspire them to join you by burning copal and sharing food or drink with them.

Pinecone Bundles

The *ocotl* pine tree was and is still used in many rites to honor those who have passed, and to help release the soul pieces of those who have passed with a pinecone *barrida* (for sweep limpia, see pages 156–158). Similar to how mourners made mummy bundle statutes of their ancestors out of pine torch, one of my Maya mentors, Don Fernando, taught me this tradition using one or four pinecones. Pine trees are associated with the

World Tree, a tripartite portal which connects the nonordinary realms or spirit realms, wherein the ancestor can be accessed. All parts of the pine tree are considered sacred, including pine needles and pinecones. Dressed pinecones are treated as the ancestor themself, and dressing the pinecone creates the ancestor and the items that are used to serve as ofrendas.

🪆 Making a Pinecone Bundle

To make a pinecone bundle with four pinecones, tie them together with a piece of cloth and place a cloth in the middle of them that will serve as a base, where most of the ofrendas will be placed. The significance of the four pinecones is connected to the cardinal spaces, and what we place in the middle of the bundle is the heart or the axis mundi. The ofrendas for a single pinecone bundle are placed in-between the wedges of the pinecone.

Dry resins, like copal, dragon's blood, frankincense, or myrrh, are burned to a liquid and then drizzled onto the pinecones. A small handful of the resins are first placed in a saucepan and covered with a carrier oil, like almond, jojoba, or sesame oil. The fire on the stove is placed on a low simmer. The resin melts in about five minutes and is then drizzled onto the pinecones. For the single pinecone bundle, dry fruit, leaves, shrubs, herbs, flowers, and feathers are used to form the eyes, nose, and make clothing and accessories for the ancestor. When it is a pinecone bundle of four, these ofrendas can be used to dress the pinecones, but they are typically placed on the cloth in-between the four pinecones.

The dressed pinecone bundle is burned on a fire pit at sunset or nighttime, as the veils of reality are thinner during these times and are ideal for our ancestors to be invoked and join in these rites. The fire also facilitates in making these ofrendas accessible to our ancestors in the nonordinary realms. It is customary to burn the pinecone bundle and honor the ancestors for four years on the day they passed, during El día de los muertos, or another day or set of days associated with the ancestor.

I personally like to sing medicine songs and play my drum as the pinecone bundle is burning. I encourage my clients to do the same, or alternatively write a love letter to their ancestor stating any requests they may have or anything they may feel guided to share with their ancestor.

Reciprocal Devotional Offerings

Devotional offerings strengthen our ancestor's soul energy, which then gives them ability to intervene on our behalf and guide us. These reciprocal devotional offerings often entail the promise to provide them with their favorite foods, flowers, or scents. Sweet smells are believed to attract our ancestors and also strengthen their soul energy with this sweetness. These reciprocal devotional offerings can also entail abstention from sex, alcohol, particular foods, or some other kind of sacrifice. Whatever the offering is, it is done for an extended period of time.

It is understood as reciprocal because by building our ancestor's soul energy through regular devotional offerings, our ancestors will reciprocate our devotion with aid, guidance, and intervention. As I described in chapter two with Elizabeth's story, we can petition their aid by leaving a petition on our ancestral altar and creating feasts of their favorite food for a regular designated period of time. I recommend nonetheless to consider making offerings regularly, such as offering water, copal, incense, or flowers. Doing so honors their soul energy and strengthens it, as well as our connection to them. This way should we do need to petition for their intervention and aid, they will be able to do so with greater expediency.

Special Days

It is also recommended to choose special days where we can celebrate our ancestors through feasts, dancing, singing, and bringing in new sacred items to the ancestral altar. This special day can include a birthday—yours or theirs—or a shared culturally significant day, such as an independence day, a holiday, or the day you felt connected to your ancestor.

When choosing a special day to celebrate an ancestor, tune into days that are special to you. There is a soul energy connection with your ancestor; strengthen it by sharing one of your special days with them.

On these special days, along with tuning into celebrations they would enjoy, share festivities that you also enjoy with your ancestor. Chances are they will enjoy them too. Sharing soul energies also often means sharing similar interests, likes, and affinities.

Traditionally, ancestral sacred spaces, such as altars, are renewed with a fire at the end of some kind of cycle, such as a birthday or annual holiday. Any of the following fire limpias can be used to renew the soul energies of your ancestor's home, their altar: a white fire limpia (see pages 38–39), placing a prayer candle on the ancestral altar also known as a *velación,* or lighting a charcoal tablet and placing copal on it.

El Día de los Muertos

The three-day celebration honoring our deceased loved ones known as El día de los muertos integrates Spanish and Mexica holy days celebrating the dead. The three days consist of the thirty-first of October, All Hallows' Eve; the first of November, All Saints Day; and the second of November, All Souls Day or the Day of the Dead. While there are variations throughout Mexico and in many parts of the United States and the Americas, as El día de los muertos is now celebrated by many, it is generally believed that at midnight on the thirty-first of October the gates of heaven open up and deceased loved ones can rejoin the world of the living through the second of November. According to Spanish traditions, it is children who rejoin the living on November 1st, and then everyone else on November 2nd.

The Spanish missionaries recognized the correlations between the feasts celebrated on the months of Tlaxochimaco and Xocotl Uetzi, the feasts of Micailhuitontli and Hueymiccaílhutl respectively, which were celebrated by the Central Mexicans in the Gregorian months of July and August. The missionaries encouraged the celebration of these feasts during these Christian holidays, but with a Mexica flare of decorating familial burials and homes with beautiful and elaborate altars that have brilliant colored *papél picado* (paper cut to make images within), ancestral skulls, calaca scenes, and various kinds of offerings: flowers, food, libations, candles, and resin.

Fig. 3.3. Marigolds, calaveras, calacas, and traditional blankets
offered to an ancestor atop this altar reminiscent of a stepped
Mesoamerican temple on October 30, 2021, at
Día de los Muertos, Altar Exhibition at Hollywood Forever.
(See also color plate 4.)
Photography by Erika Buenaflor.

It is customary to make more public temporary ancestral altars during these holidays. In many spaces throughout Mexico and in the Southwest, breathtaking colorful ancestral altars decorate cemeteries, parks, and other community spaces. These altars, of course, are not always public demonstrations of honoring our deceased loved ones; they can also be created in homes or other private spaces and can be completely or partially dismantled after this holiday. The items that are used to create these altars can include all the items that were discussed in chapter two (see pages 67–70), and can be scenes relevant to that ancestor, such as a room from the deceased, a special party, or a funeral procession (see figures 3.3 and 3.4).

The manner in which the contemporary Yucatec Maya celebrate the Day of the Dead, also known by them as *Hanal Pixan* (Food of the Souls) reflects some of the unique Maya customs and traditions. Along with the decorating familial burials and homes with extravagant altars, it is customary to clean the house and wash all of the laundry before the celebrations. They may also tie a red or black ribbon around the right wrist of children to prevent the spirits from taking them, and they tie up dogs to allow the spirits of ancestors to freely pass through the house undisturbed. Most importantly, they make foods that are unique to the Maya area of the Yucatán Peninsula, such as *múkbil* ("to put in the ground" or to cook in a *pib,* an "underground oven"), accompanied by a cup of *atole.* The múkbil is much larger than a normal tamale and is made with corn and lard dough stuffed with chicken and pork meat, tomato, and peppers, then wrapped in banana leaves and cooked in an underground pit with firewood and stones. An extra plate of the delicious traditional Maya food is often placed at the altar for their deceased loved ones and also for the deceased souls that maybe no one remembers and need somewhere to dine.

Tune into whether honoring your ancestor with a unique plate of food, papél picado, special scented candle, delicious chocolates, or an additional altar for this holiday resonates with you.

Fig. 3.4. An ancestor honored with a bounty of fruit and flowers
surrounding La Virgen de Guadalupe up to Jesus on the cross on
October 30, 2021, at Día de los Muertos, Altar Exhibition
at Hollywood Forever. (See also color plate 5.)
Photography by Erika Buenaflor.

Trance Dancing, Singing, and Spoken Word

Invite your ancestors to dance or sing with or through you. Personally, I find using or listening to some kind of percussion very helpful to flow in the pure energy of a dance or song. If I am dancing, I will engage in gazing by having my eyes one-tenth open, which is conducive for trance or meditative states. I may also wear white or lighter colors or clothes that help me to feel lighter or more conducive to trance dancing. When I am singing, different auditory sounds may come out, pitches and tones that sound nothing like my usual voice, and I just allow them to come forth.

The spoken word has also been traditionally understood by our Mesoamerican ancestors as an ofrenda. Take space and time to write a poem, story, or spoken word for your ancestor. When it is completed, light a charcoal tablet, place some copal on it, invite your ancestor, and share your spoken word with them. The very act of engaging in creative writing ventures for or with our ancestors moves us deeper in those trance creative spaces, spaces of consciousness that intersect with other realms, the spaces where we connect with our ancestors.

Communing with Our Ancestors in Nature or Taking a Trip

The peace and calmness of being out in nature often helps us to connect from within and receive messages from our ancestors. Take a nature walk, go on a hike, and if you have access to a body of water, like the ocean, enjoy it! Before beginning your trail or walking on the sand make an offering, such as homegrown sage or tobacco, or send love to this space. When you embark out in nature, take a moment to listen to the sounds of nature and take them in. In this space of tranquility, call in your ancestor to connect with you. Before leaving thank your ancestor and all of nature for joining you.

Consider also taking a trip to a sacred site or place that helps you feel more connected to your ancestors. Energetic imprints of our ancestors are on the land, buildings, temples, and art. Engage in some conscious breathwork, thank your ancestors for joining you, and allow yourself to feel the energy and magic of these spaces. Imagine the ceremonies and festivities that may have been taking place, and let the energy of these spaces themselves, along with your ancestors, teach and help you to reconnect.

AN ANCESTOR INTERVENES TO CLEAR AN ANCESTRAL CURSE

Beth, a younger grandmother of one grandchild and a mother of two daughters, first came to me for a divination reading focusing on how to heal her estranged family. Her family was no longer on speaking terms. According to her, the women in her ancestral lineage were plagued by being with men that engaged in constant cycles of betrayal and sexual infidelity.

It started with Beth's mom, who passed in her early forties due to a stroke. Throughout her life, her mother had gone through cycles of depression and was incapable of being tender with her children because of her father's constant infidelity. According to Beth, her mom died due to a broken heart. Beth intended to shift this cycle but believed that her daughters had inherited this possible curse.

Beth became pregnant with her first daughter Rosie during her senior year in high school at age seventeen. She moved in with the father's parents, as her mother was not strong enough to provide assistance. She had Mary a couple of years later. The girls' father was repeatedly unfaithful to her and unable to hold a job for more than eight months. He preferred smoking marijuana and drinking to being a partner or suitable father to his daughters. After catching him in yet another act of infidelity, Beth finally left him when the girls were seven (Rosie) and five (Mary).

Beth worked full-time as a secretary and put herself through college. She became an elementary teacher, as she thought this career would afford her the opportunity to be close to her daughters. She set out to be a good role model for her daughters as well as a strong, independent provider, especially since their father remained absent by choice.

Although Beth's family of three were close and happy with one another, this changed when Rosie was seventeen. Rosie became pregnant after graduating high school, so Beth encouraged Rosie's boyfriend to move in with them and told them that she would help them as a family. Mark, a very charismatic and charming young man, worked full-time while going to community college. He lived with them without any incidents for over a year, until a few months after Rosie had given birth to their baby, when Mark was unfaithful.

The household became fractured when Mary, Rosie's sister, caught Mark talking with and then kissing another woman, but Mark convinced Mary not to divulge it to Rosie at the first sign of trouble. By the time Mary did talk to Rosie about it, it led to a blowout argument between the girls. With her daughters not speaking to one another, Beth asked Mark to leave.

A few weeks later, Mark persuaded Rosie to move in with his family. He convinced her that it was a one-time incident and he would not make the same mistake. He also turned Rosie against her family, telling her Beth would not allow them to be happy. Beth was brokenhearted because she had not seen her granddaughter since this fiasco began.

There was also tension between Beth and Mary because Mary felt Beth should have stood up for her. When Mary moved out and went away to college in Northern California a few months later, she became more distant.

Beth tried to reconcile her relationship with both of her daughters, but Rosie was not speaking to her and Mary continued her distance. With a few exceptions of cold, brief, or angry conversations with her daughters, it had been almost six months since Beth had spoken to her daughters or sat with them as a family.

Learning of Beth's history, I sensed that there may have been an ancestral curse thrown at the women in her family. In our first session, I offered her I Am presence clearing of ancestral curses and brought in the I Am presence of her daughters to offer them this clearing as well. I can always call in the I Am presence of someone through their parents or loved ones to receive these gifts. It is presented as an offering to their I Am, and the I Am always accepts what is ideal for us.

To heal this lineage, I asked Beth to create an ancestral altar for the women in her family, and to do a velación in the form of a circle to influence outcomes (see figure 3.5). I asked her to write a petition on a parchment paper with a number 2 pencil, asking that anything less than love and light between her, her daughters, and them as a family be transmuted with and by the Sacred Fires of God's Love and Light. On top of this petition, she would place a saint candle—I recommended Our Lady of Guadalupe to help inspire compassion and love between her family—and next to the saint candle she would have a glass of water and a cracked egg inside the glass. She would light the seven-day candle with a wooden stick match, without using her breath to blow it out, and repeat this with the other eight white candles circling the principal saint candle and do so in a clockwise manner. She would let the candles

CIRCLES

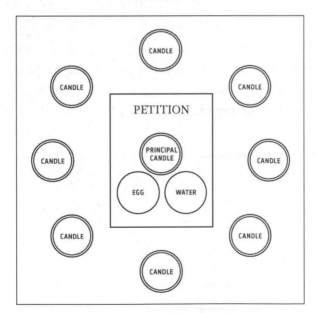

CIRCLE TO INFLUENCE AN OUTCOME.

Fig. 3.5. Drawing of a velación in the form of a
circle to influence outcomes.
Drawing by Carolina Gutierrez.

burn without extinguishing them. I told her to do this and start on the next full moon.

In our next session, Beth told me that the principal saint candle turned black and showed me a picture. From the looks of the picture, the glasses from a few other candles also looked gray. Beth told me that the morning after the last candle went out, her daughter Mary called her. Mary had a nightmare that her mother was sick in the hospital and became worried. Although Beth still felt that Mary was distant in the phone conversation, she personally felt lighter. Beth shared with me that Mary used to always laugh with her, and they would constantly make each other laugh, but this had not happened since the incident with Mark.

Beth told me that she kept having dreams and physical interactions with spiders. We both felt that due to their multiple interactions in dreams and the ways they kept coming around, the spiders were giving Beth spider medicine, healing, and weaving back the women in her family. I tuned into this and I felt it was a grandmother Maya creator deity, Xmucane, often depicted as a spider weaving woman. After a Mesoamerican divination card reading, we received confirmation that a great-great-grandmother of Beth's was asking to connect with Beth, and together they would heal the women in their line.

I asked Beth to include weaving instruments—loom, yarn, comb, and powerful images of spider deities and spider medicine on her altar. Thereafter, I asked to repeat the velación on the peak of the waning moon to transmute obstacles. I also asked her to engage in a cacao ceremony after she lit the last candle to connect with her great-great-grandmother, offer her healing, and thank her for healing the relationships with the women in her family.

In our next session, Beth told me that the glasses in her next velación were completely clear. She also shared with me that she felt the presence of her great-great-grandmother giving her strength and guiding her each day. A few days after the new moon after her velación, she received a call from Rosie, who wanted to arrange a meeting in the next month so Beth could see and spend time with her granddaughter, Karla.

Plate 1. Shows the diverse offerings—food, jewels, clothing, mirrors, blankets, and ceramics—made specifically to a merchant ancestor. These items not only ensured their comfort and well-being but also enabled them to continue their trade as merchants in the afterlife.
Courtesy of Ancient Americas at LACMA. Codex Magliabechiano plate 68r.

Plate 2. Depicts the funeral of a ruler as a bundle going into a fiery pit of cremation, the offerings that were being included in the cremation, and the Mexica's somber crying ceremonies. These wailing ceremonies enabled the release of the ancestor's soul energies and also were fundamental in the healing and release of the families.
Courtesy of Ancient Americas at LACMA. Codex Magliabechiano, plate 67r.

Plate 3. Burning copal fills the air with smoke, the lilies with fragrance. I give them offerings of food and my deepest love and respect through my own permanent ancestral altar.

Photography by Erika Buenaflor.

Plate 4. Marigolds, calaveras, calacas, and traditional blankets offered to an ancestor atop this altar reminiscent of a stepped Mesoamerican temple on October 30, 2021, at Día de los Muertos, Altar Exhibition at Hollywood Forever. *Photography by Erika Buenaflor.*

Plate 5. An ancestor honored with a bounty of fruit and flowers surrounding
La Virgen de Guadalupe up to Jesus on the cross on October 30, 2021,
at Día de los Muertos, Altar Exhibition at Hollywood Forever.
Photography by Erika Buenaflor.

Plate 6. Calacas paid their respects to the grave of a newly deceased ancestor. Honored with crosses and corn on October 30, 2021, at Día de los Muertos, Altar Exhibition at Hollywood Forever.
Photography by Erika Buenaflor.

Plate 7. Just beyond the portal of the feathered serpent sat Aztec royalty attended by his servant in a magnificent display on October 30, 2021, at Día de los Muertos, Altar Exhibition at Hollywood Forever.
Photography by Erika Buenaflor.

Plate 8. A jovial scene took place as calacas sang and played music together in a timber-framed building surrounded by many photos of friends and family on October 30, 2021, at Día de los Muertos, Altar Exhibition at Hollywood Forever. *Photography by Erika Buenaflor.*

Plate 9. An artistic expression of the separation of animating energies at death—teyolía, tonalli, and ihiyotl. At the head, a serpent's head appears, representing the tonalli. Another serpent head protrudes out from the stomach/liver, representing the ihiyotl. From the chest, the face of Ehécatl-Quetzalcóatl comes out, which corresponds to the teyolía.
Codex Laud pg. 44. Drawing by Carolina Gutierrez.

A few days after that, Mary called her with good news about getting straight A's in all of her midterms. For the first time in months, Mary laughed, even joked, just like before. Beth cried tears of joy as she laughed with her daughter.

Beth's homework was to engage in shamanic dancing with her great-great-grandmother on the next full moon, utilizing the Night Sun energies of transformation and the full moon energies of completion and manifestation. Beth was unsure what music would be suitable. But she felt ranchero music, where she could howl a good *hiiy-hiiy-hiiy* from the top of her lungs, would be good for her soul. I agreed that this was perfect, and I still asked her to please cleanse the space, make an offering of copal, and thank her great-great-grandmother once again for helping her heal the relationships between her and her daughters. And then, invite her great-great-grandmother to sing and dance through her and have fun!

In our next session, Beth seemed much more at peace. She told me that a couple weeks after this performance and before her meeting with Rosie and Karla, Rosie called her mom sobbing because Mark was still involved with the other woman. Rosie and Karla moved back home at that point. Rosie and Mary also spoke on the phone a month after that and cried while apologizing to each other.

That next Christmas they celebrated as a family together and had a plate prepared for their great-great-grandmother and even had gifts for her altar. Her daughters wholeheartedly accepted her as their ancestor, and as a family they engage in ancestral veneration rituals. I have also been blessed to meet her daughters in person in sessions; they are on a path of great self-love and self-acceptance and are now determined to develop and trust their intuition, especially when it comes to their romantic partners.

CHAPTER 4

Rebirth, Renewal, and Continuation of Our Ancestors

The soul energies of our ancestors can be reborn, renewed, and continued in many ways. We can engage in ceremonies to invite them to infuse their soul energies into our altars, the sacred items we place on our ancestral altars and have elsewhere, and our ancestral bundles. They can also infuse us with their soul energies in times and spaces we may need them or when we connect with them by honoring them in ceremonies or by studying about them.

One of the first times I experienced this infusion of soul energy from my Mesoamerican ancestors was the first day in one of my Xicanx studies classes at the University of California at Los Angeles (UCLA) with the late Professor Gómez-Quiñones. There was a huge part of me that felt greatly intimidated by attending UCLA, especially because I was one of the very few students that was living on her own, working full-time as a waitress, and enrolled as a full-time student. I felt out of place and was not yet confident in my intellectual skills. On this day, Professor Gómez-Quiñones passed around a map of Tenochtitlan, the capital of the Aztec empire, to all the students. He asked us to tell him what we could tell about the people by strictly looking at the layout of the capital. As he was poking fun at students for putting "too much salsa" on their descriptions, something incredible happened to me. As I was looking at the map, a bright white light flashed in my third eye and I remembered. I remembered the spiritual and agricultural significance of why we had *chinampas* (floating gardens) in certain areas, the significances of the city crossways that mimicked the Aztec Sun calendar, the temples we had in certain areas and why, and memories that I am still integrating to this day. And, yes, I was completely sober, and no, that had never happened to me before, although it was definitely not the last time I would experience this. This white light was an incredible infusion of energy from my Mesoamerican ancestors generally. I became completely confident in myself and began to delve into my roots with great passion and deep love. I later graduated summa cum laude with college honors.

I experienced a large degree of ancestral soul energy about nine years later, after my 2005 catastrophic injury.* I was in Las Vegas for a work convention and decided to go to Red Rock Canyon. On the day of my hike, I found the spot that called me and went into a deep journey. When I came out of the journey, I realized four hours had passed, although it only felt like fifteen minutes. Unfortunately, I jumped up, panicking, and did not take time to ground myself. I slipped and fell over thirty feet. The fall resulted in a skull fracture, brain hemorrhage, left acromioclavicular joint separation, two fractured vertebrae, shattered coccyx, three fractures in the left leg, and a right leg fractured down from the knee, with my bones coming out of my heel. I also experienced severe osteomyelitis, lost half the bones in my right ankle, and almost had my right foot amputated. I was told I would be in pain the rest of my life, and if I walked again, it would likely be with some kind of assistance. I decided in the hospital to finally fully embrace my *don* (healing gift from God), step into my power, and learn to stop doubting intuitive divine guidance (the most difficult of all).

When I finally came home, I was still in a wheelchair, but I was able to start using a walker even though I was still not able to place pressure on my right foot. Fortunately, using a walker allowed me to begin my sacred gardening. Prior to this accident, I had been mentoring for almost seven years with my first two curanderx mentors, Don Tomas,

---

*I discuss the accident, my healing journey, and mentorship in greater detail in my first book, *Cleansing Rites of Curanderismo*.

who taught me a lot about facilitating limpias and working with plants, and Barbara,* who was a *sobadera,* and taught me about moving and diagnosing energy in the physical and subtle bodies (a.k.a. aura), among other things. During my recovery period, I put into practice everything I had learned from my mentors and allowed myself to work intuitively. Don Tomas first taught me about the many ways our ancestor's energies could be reborn. He had a lime tree that his grandmother blessed with her soul energy. The lime limpias he performed that came from this tree were amazing and could clear any blocks imaginable.

Along with moving any stuck energy and stimulating my muscles and joints with breathwork, intent, and stimulating acupressure points, I decided to work with herbs and avocado leaves that I knew were going to help support my joints and ease my pain. I wrote a petition and left it on my ancestral altar welcoming my ancestors to infuse their soul energies into the petition as well as the herbs and avocado tree leaves I would later use to make tinctures to strengthen my joints, muscles, and ensure my impeccable recovery. I placed a single, seven-day prayer candle of Our Lady of Guadalupe on top of my petition and began the velación on the full moon. (I discuss in greater detail the ritual aspects of this ceremony on pages 115–118). On the next new moon, I burned my petition and made little holes in the soil, dispersing the ashes of my petition into my rue, lemon balm, lavender, chamomile, and avocado tree. Fortunately, I had an area where I had potted herbs, so this ceremony was fairly easy to do in my walker. For the next full moon, I picked leaves from the herbs and avocado tree and made a tincture. While I was engaging in many healing limpia rituals, I had a strong sense that my ancestors blessed these plants and me with their soul energies. Although I was in a wheelchair for almost a year and could not place pressure on my right foot, after my last surgery, I was able to walk with a completely normal gait in less than two weeks.

According to ancient Mesoamericans, the soul-animating energies of our ancestors could be reborn, renewed, and continued in many diverse,

---

*I tried to address Barbara and my latter mentor, Malina, as doña before their first names, which is customary and is a sign of respect. But they refused, and of course, I respected that.

multifaceted ways. Aspects or all of an ancestor's soul energies could be reborn into one of their heirs or a fruit or vegetable orchard; they could also infuse their essence into insects on particular days, or become a bird, hummingbird, or butterfly. At death, rulers, for example, were believed to have particularly strong soul-animating energies, and their expressions could become manifestations of the sacred, other deified ancestors, deities, and cosmic World Trees, or they could participate in cosmic cycles and could become the embodiment and personification of the calendrical cycles being celebrated.[1] Their soul energies could also possibly reside in different nonordinary realms in the afterlife, giving them more authority to aid and intervene on their heir's behalf.

The honoring and strengthening of our ancestor's soul energy is reciprocal. Through ancestral veneration rites, every time we strengthen their soul energies, we also strengthen our soul energies. I will draw from ancient Mesoamerican wisdom and expand on ancestral veneration rites that are aimed at engaging in raising our soul energies reciprocally, and also aid us in deepening our connections with our ancestors. I will also delve into how one of my clients encouraged the continuation of her grandmother into her roses, and her life, and ensured that her grandmother, as her ancestor, had stronger soul energy to intervene and help her.

INHERITING ANCESTRAL SOUL ENERGY

For the ancient Maya, the terms *k'uh* or *ch'u* could refer both to a specific god or to the general quality of sacredness.[2] This concept was extended through the related word *k'uhul*, which referred to soul-animating energy that emanated from deities, ancestors, and the cosmos. This energy was present throughout the world and pervaded the Earth and all of her inhabitants, including humans, animals, plants, sacred objects, the elements, and the landscape. The ancient Maya also conceptualized different manifestations of animating soul energy. Maya artwork and early ethnohistorical records suggest that this soul energy was also concentrated in certain regions of the body, which likely included the head, heart, blood, and breath.[3]

Both Classic and modern Maya notions of soul energies, death, and ancestors emphasize themes of rebirth, renewal, continuation of soul energies, and indicate that babies can be born or later invigorated with an esteemed ancestor's soul energy.[4] Ancestors with strong soul energies would await cycle(s) before being reborn, like the Sun.[5] Rulers often claimed that the spirits or soul energies of deities, animals, and ancestors were reborn in them and took on their names.[6] This auspicious ancestral soul energy was transferred into the ruler in their naming ceremonies. Naming was associated with the head, the seat of identity, likely the soul-animating energy associated with the head.[7] Ancestral soul energy was also likely transferred into newborns in the naming aspect of the bathing rites of newborns.

Many contemporary Maya still believe that when a grandparent's name is given to a child, the grandparent's soul energy is recycled or transferred into the child.[8] Receiving the soul of an ancestor is also a widespread Maya concept known as *k'ex* or *k'exel*.[9] It is associated with the transfer and continuity of human life and is manifest in the common practice of "replacing" or "substituting" an older or deceased person, especially a grandparent, by giving a child born in their family the same name.[10]

The Tzotzil Maya of Zinacantán believe that after death, the soul (*ch'ulel*) eventually rejoins a pool of souls that are cared for by the ancestral gods and is later placed into a newborn to give life to another person. The Yucatec Maya believe that all souls, wicked or not, eventually return to earth to be reincarnated in newborns.[11] The K'iche' believe that on *Cib*—or as they call it, *Ahmac*, "a day sign of their divinatory calendar when their ancestors can take the form of an insect called *ahmak*." On this day, they make offerings to the souls of their ancestors and ask them to visit their homes.[12]

EXPANSIVE SOUL-ANIMATING ENERGIES

The quality of the ancestor's soul energies at death typically correlated with the day of birth, social class, age, and how well the individual preserved their soul energies during their life.[13] At death, ancestral rulers and those of social importance became the special dead. They were perceived as having stronger and more expansive soul energies that could become deified ancestors, traverse nonordinary realms, control the natural elements, and influence circumstances to their will. Their heirs engaged in numerous ancestral veneration rites to continue to strengthen their ancestor's soul energies to ensure their renewal, rebirth, continuance, and ability to intervene on their behalf.

Common artistic tropes expressing the expansive nature of an ancestor's soul energy, particularly royal soul energy, include:

1. Their rebirth as plants of economic and symbolic import, such as maize and cacao
2. Their renascence as or as aspects of the often-cyclical nature of the Maize Deity
3. A deathly voyage through water and along roads
4. Their transformation as animating soul energies, portrayed as inspiriting winds
5. As an axis mundi depicted as a world tree or transference and ascension through a world tree
6. Their afterlife in royal abodes filled with food, drink, and offerings
7. Imagery of their solar apotheosis or some other cosmic renewal[14]

At the Burial 9 at El Zotz, the temple's stucco depicts the ancestral ruler as the Sun in all of his aspects, subject to daily renewal, but also cloaked and transformed at night against a celestial band.[15] The artwork on various bowls left inside the tomb attests to the bond between rulers and resurgent recycling diurnal and seasonal Suns. Monkeys bellow the coming of the dawn Sun, while old gods shapeshift into turtles that float into islands on distant seas, depicting the ruler in his day and night aspects as the Sun.[16]

The west side Stela C of Copan depicts ancestral ruler Waxaklahun Ubah K'awil as the World Tree, and as the World Tree he helps to support the cosmos and sustain creation. On both faces of Stela C, he grasps double-headed serpent bars representative of the celestial sky or Upperworld. From the serpents' maws, ancestors come out from the outer limits of the stela. The lower portion of the east side of Stela C has him in the form of a crocodile tree emerging from a mountain. His loin apron becomes the trunk of the World Tree, while serpents, often associated with the sky, extend out both sides, forming his branches.[17]

Many contemporary Maya (such as the Tzeltal and Tzoltzil) and Classic Maya recognize crosses or World Trees as conduits by which soul energies travel during dreams or in death.[18] One well-known example is ancestral ruler Pakal's stone sarcophagus lid, which depicts his departure out of the Underworld and his resurrection, regeneration, and rebirth. The resurrected ruler rises up along a World Tree, which acts as an axis mundi or portal that transfers his body to a Flowery Realm in the Upperworld. Pakal wears the symbols of the Sun god, and like the Sun, he will be reborn at dawn.[19] His sarcophagus lid functioned as a container for Pakal's remains and a vehicle for his rebirth.[20]

The sarcophagus lid also portrays Pakal's royal ancestors emerging from the earth as animated fruit trees.[21] Ten named ancestor portraits are depicted in stucco on the tomb walls, enabling them to oversee his interment and watch over his tomb for eternity.[22] The imagery of the ancestors as animating fruit trees depicts the understanding that upon death ancestors transformed into the riches of the earth.[23] Pakal was positioned as a cosmic centerpiece primed for resurrection into the world of his ancestors.[24]

Dressed as the Maize Deity, along with his solar apotheosis, Pakal's soul energies or aspects of it would undergo cyclical resurgence as the Maize Deity, who was often depicted as undergoing ongoing cycles of rebirth, life, and death.[25] Pakal's body, his regalia, and the inside of his sarcophagus were all also covered in red cinnabar. Placing red cinnabar over the bodies of their ancestors ensured their continuing prestige and distinction in the afterlife.[26] The psychoduct that snaked through the pyramid's inner stairs and into Pakal's burial chamber enabled his heirs' communication, access, and practices of ancestral veneration rites.[27] The sacred artwork of the sarcophagus lid and the tomb, his sacred accoutrements, and the subsequent ancestral veneration rites also held at the mouth of the psychoduct facilitated the rebirth, vitality, and continuity of Pakal and his royal ancestors.

The other two known Maya sarcophagi are from Classic-period Tonina, Palenque's chief rival. The Tonina sarcophagi were found in vaulted tombs below the open plaza floor of Terrace 5.[28] At Tonina the sarcophagus tombs were accessible in light of their shallow placement below Terrace 5. There are a number of hieroglyphic references to tomb reentry at the site, likely for ancestral veneration rites.[29]

The Maya Classic-period Berlin Vase depicts the funeral of the rebirth and renewal of a Maya ruler, who at his death has gone through a metamorphosis as the Maize Deity and ancestral cacao trees and has experienced a solar apotheosis. On one side of the vessel (right side of Fig. 4.1, page 110) the ruler is evidencing a rebirth as the Maize Deity with maize growth that spills over his bundled corpse. Above the bundled ruler there appears to be the first glyph *bih* (road) with netted maize imagery on the sides of the road and a floating head of the Sun God with his day and night aspects on opposite sides, suggesting his solar apotheosis. At the forehead is a burning or animating *ajaw* face (the ajaw face is depicted with two dots as the eyes and a third dot at the bottom as the mouth), indicating that the ruler's animating soul energies have entered the celestial path of souls. On the opposite side (left side of the drawing) the ruler has been reduced to bones and has been reborn as cacao trees sprouting from his tomb.[30] The vessel shows the multifaceted expressions of continuance and renewal of the ruler's soul-animating energies.

Inside the tombs of rulers and the elite, figurines and jade beads were also placed within *Spondylus* shells, implying that these ancestors, as seeds of animating energy, would be reborn from the husk of a shell. A *Spondylus* shell from Burial 13 at Piedras Negras was incised with the glyph *ik'* (wind or breath), suggesting its animate value.[31] *Spondylus* and maize were symbolically linked as common Maya symbols for life and

Fig. 4.1 Depicts the funeral of the rebirth and renewal of a Maya ruler,
who at his death has gone through a metamorphosis as the maize deity
and ancestral cacao trees and has experienced a solar apotheosis.
Courtesy of Ancient Americas at LACMA. Berlin Vase, vessel K6547. SD-5503.
Rollout drawing by Nikolai Grube. Drawing by Mark Van Stone.
Copyright © David Schele.

vitality. Jade beads were understood as seeds of new life, *Spondylus* as
the shell or husk that contained it.[32]

POSTCLASSIC CENTRAL MEXICO

For the Postclassic Central Mexicans, the death of an ancestor, especially a ruler or leader of the community, typically resulted in a rebirth,
renewal, or continuance of their soul-animating energies. These soul-
animating energies were continuously self-generating and transforming,
especially with ancestral veneration rites that acted as catalysts for the
different expressions of their animating energies. Deities embodied different clusters of specific animating energies and endowed humans with
these sacred energies at different periods of their lives and for different
reasons, including: during the baby bathing rite ceremony, when coura-
geous feats were accomplished in war, at state ceremonial community
performances, and when individuals turned fifty-two years old.[33]

    At the bathing rite ceremony, the *temixiuitiani, tietl,* or *tlamatqui*
(midwife) divined a child's name and fate; the name was a family name

that was believed to confer ancestral tonalli to the child.[34] Inheriting an ancestral family name ensured that ancestral tonalli could be passed from generation to generation.[35] Nahuatl-language names were not immediately displaced by Spanish ones in colonial central Mexico; rather, they were often retained and served as a second name until the late sixteenth century.[36]

At death, ancestors did not perish, but through their soul energies began to live again as different expressions of existence.[37] Alfredo López Austin interprets page 44 from the Codex Laud as an artistic expression of the separation of animating energies at death (see figure 4.2). At the head, a serpent's head appears, representing the tonalli. Another serpent head protrudes out from the stomach/liver, representing the ihiyotl. From the chest, the face of Ehécatl-Quetzalcóatl comes out, which would

Fig. 4.2. An artistic expression of the separation of animating energies at death—teyolía, tonalli, and ihiyotl. At the head, a serpent's head appears, representing the tonalli. Another serpent head protrudes out from the stomach/liver, representing the ihiyotl. From the chest, the face of Ehécatl-Quetzalcóatl comes out, which corresponds to the teyolía.
(See also color plate 9.)
Codex Laud pg. 44. Drawing by Carolina Gutierrez.

correspond to the teyolía.[38] There remains an animated skeletonized figure, composed of the skull and spine, which as indicated in chapter two may have retained aspects of the ancestor's soul-animating energies, yet these animating energies were generally not bound to the earthly realms.

When the Mexica placed the green stone, the *chalchíhuitl*, with the dead body or cremated ashes, the stone heart attracted the soul pieces to the inert ash or bone fragments. This ensured that the deceased would not wander to disturb the living. If one was cremated, relatives would gather up all the ashes, a green stone with two locks of hair—one from birth and the other upon death—and place them into an earthen vessel or box. They then placed a wooden figure on it that represented the image of the ancestor, buried it, and continued to make offerings at the place it was buried.[39] The *chalchíhuitl* lent its own animating power and sustained the vitality of the ancestor's remains.[40] The locks of hair were included because they were believed to contain the soul energy upon birth and death and acted like magnets to attract the remaining soul energy of the deceased wherever it was to be found.[41] This ceremony was the *quitonaltía,* which was intended to strengthen the ancestor's soul energy.[42]

At death, an ancestor's tonalli remained near the body for four days in order to retrieve all of the pieces of itself on Earth. On the fourth day after death, at the time of cremation, the ancestor's teyolía left the world of the living and journeyed into the realms of the afterlife.[43] Cremation was the standard procedure for transmitting the teyolía to the afterlife.[44] The souls of dead children went to Chichihualcuauhco, likely understood as a favorable afterlife where these children were nourished by the breasts that hung from a vibrant tree[45] Those who were called by Tlaloc, the principal rain deity, and died from phenomena associated with water went to Tlalocan, an earthly paradise of green plants and unending springtime.[46] The souls of people who died of old age, natural causes, diseases, accidents, or other circumstances not specified by the gods went to the Underworld, Mictlampa, or a cold, barren area with extensive plains and open deserts, a place of uncertainty and possibilities for regenerative gifts.[47] Warriors, rulers, and nobility went to Xochitlan, a paradisal land of flowers situated in the Upperworld.[48]

The burning of funerary bundles at Teotihuacán and with the later Mexica reflected the concept of the metamorphosed butterfly accompanying the reborn Sun at dawn.[49] In Teotihuacán, Toltec, and Mexica art, warriors were frequently represented as butterflies and wore butterfly headdresses and nosepieces. A common Toltec warrior emblem was a large butterfly pectoral made of turquoise. Mexica warriors also often wore large butterfly images on their backs as insignias. In the funerary rituals of Teotihuacán and the Mexica, fire served as the transformative process for the metamorphosis and resurrection of the warrior soul.[50]

The annual ritual burning of effigies of the ancestor, which lasted four years, gave the ancestor more opportunities to attract and recover more fragments of their tonalli.[51] The teyolía could also exist in different nonordinary realms and their levels. When discussing the funeral of Mexica ruler Axayácatl, Diego Durán, a sixteenth-century ethnohistorian, mentions that the ruler could be found in the Underworld, Mictlan, and in the Upperworld, House of the Sun.[52] This ancestral ruler had stronger soul-animating energies and at death could express his animating energies in different realms.[53] After four years, warriors, rulers, and —nobility— those with stronger soul-animating energies—would become birds, hummingbirds, and butterflies and spend an eternity drinking the nectar of flowers both in the heavenly realm of the Sun and on Earth.[54]

INTEGRATING ANCIENT MESOAMERICAN WISDOM

Strengthening of Soul Energies

Every time we engage in an ancestral veneration rite, as elaborate or simple and sweet as it may be, we strengthen the soul-animating energies of our ancestors. The following ancestral veneration ceremonies are to strengthen their soul energies—and oftentimes ours, so that our ancestors may take a more active role in our lives continuing their existence in designated sacred spaces, items, and ways, and intervene and guide us toward soul medicine.

Rebirth into Our Garden and Plants

There are many ways we can continue to strengthen the soul energies of our ancestors, and one viable way we can encourage their rebirth, revitalization, and continuance is by inviting their soul energy to grow in our gardens or plants. In doing so, we are playing the role of gardener parterx (midwife). In this guise of parterx, death of an ancestor is not the end; rather, we are facilitating the rebirth, renewal, and continuance of their sacred energy into our gardens. If we have edible plants in our gardens, then we are definitely facilitating not only a stronger connection with our ancestors, but also allowing our soul energies and physical bodies to be strengthened with their soul energies.

If we have the ashes of our ancestors, we can disperse them in various ways, including placing them in our gardens. Before doing so, ask your ancestor what kind of plant or tree they may want to come back as. Remember to also share with them your understanding of the gifts of plants and trees and tune into what feels ideal all the way around.

As trees, they can become world trees in our physical spaces, letting their roots tap into the gifts and wisdom of the Underworld—tenacity, persistence, courageousness, and humility. Their trunks and bodies can connect with the gifts and wisdom of the Middleworld—bounty, fertility, and renewal. Their branches can access the gifts of the Upperworld—rebirth, resurrection, and transformation. Every time we connect with our ancestors, we can connect with these wisdoms and gifts. As fruit trees, they can also share soul energies as the sweetness of the fruit.

Flowers spread joy, happiness, hope, and have incredibly wonderful healing properties. Is there a flower you see them becoming? Herbs, along with often having numerous healing properties, have extraordinary cleansing properties. Do you see them providing healing and cleansing for you—your family, living spaces, and sacred spaces—as herbs? Vegetables provide nourishment, can strengthen our immune system, cleanse our body of free radicals, and do so much more. Do you see your ancestor providing food for you and your family? Cacti and succulents are continuously recycling energies for us, along with providing healing for our bodies. Do you see your ancestor aiding you with transmuting any dense energies in your living spaces? They can also become a part of the grass, palms, and decorative plants.

Connecting with Plants

Take some deep intentional breaths and journey into your sacred heart to connect with your ancestor (see pages 37–44). Share with them how you see the plants in your living spaces and ask them if they would like to be reborn as one of these plants or trees. You can go through the list of plants and see if you get a "yes" or "no," or you can tune into which choice you feel gives you some kind of energy surge. Once you perceive your ancestor has determined an ideal way for them to share space with you in your garden or among your plants, then it is time to prepare for this sacred rebirthing ceremony.

If you do not have the ash of your ancestor's actual remains, then you can use the ash of a picture of them or a metaphorical picture—a picture that you feel embodies them or connects you to them—or a petition. Write this petition ideally on the evening of a full moon.* In this petition, share with your ancestor why you would love for them to share the space with you in the garden embodied as whichever plant(s) or tree(s) you felt were ideal. If it seems appropriate, please also share how you would love them to help guide you in your life and anything else you feel is appropriate. Once you are done writing the petition, place it on your altar or somewhere special.

On the night of the full moon, place a seven-day prayer candle on top of your petition, light the candle with a matchstick, and gently shake the match until the fire goes out. Keep in mind that seven-day candles usually burn out before the seven days. Do not snuff out your candle. If you are concerned about leaving something lit, consider placing the candle in a water mug and placing the petition underneath the water mug.

Make daily offerings of copal or incense to the ashes of your ancestor, their picture, or the petition you used to charge with your ancestor's soul

---

*As I explain in my third book, *Sacred Energies of the Sun and Moon*, the energies of the full moon and Night Sun emit completion, manifestation, and transformation.

energies, from the time of the full moon (or the time your candle burns out if you used a petition) to the next new moon. Every morning, take a moment to connect with the morning sun, and thank the morning sun for giving your picture or petition tonalli and also infusing it with the soul energy of your ancestor (the ashes presumably already have the soul energies of your ancestor). In the evenings, thank the Night Sun for helping the soul energy of your ancestor transform and become a part of your garden—plant(s) or tree(s). Thank the waning moon for aiding you in your role as a parterx. In the meantime, prepare the area(s) for planting by clearing any brush and making a nice hole where you will later bury the ashes of your ancestor, picture, or petition. If you do not have a garden, this can be done within the soil of your favorite house plants; just be careful when making a small hole so you do not hurt the root system of the plant.

On the morning of the new moon, read and burn your petition or picture, whichever one you decided to use. You can burn them in the pot as a white fire limpia (see pages 38–39). The energies of the new moon and morning sun emit rebirth and creation, which are ideal to foster a sacred space for your ancestor to rebirth into as a plant. The fire carries the energy or message of your petition to your ancestor in the nonordinary realms. That evening, bury the ashes next to a plant or tree.

Next time you sit, pick, or eat the fruit or vegetables of where your ancestor was buried, thank your ancestor for energizing and revitalizing your garden, plant(s), tree(s), and you with their soul energy.

Velaciones with a Candle

Fire in the form of a velación can serve as a link between us and our ancestors. The flickering candles repel unwanted spiritual beings and energies from a situation and serve as a portal for our ancestor to enter into our realm. In this case, the fire is inviting your ancestor to charge your petition with your ancestor's soul energies. While any candle can be used, seven-day candles are fairly easy to divine into particular situations and the current probable outcomes. The clearer the glass is after the candle goes out, the more graceful and favorable outcomes are indicated. If the glass turns gray or dark, the darker color is generally an indication of a clearing of an ancestral curse (or another layer of it) or a clearing of negative thoughts or energy sent your way concerning this situation. If the fire goes out, this is typically an indication that you need to clear and bolster your energies. In the latter two situations, I recommend getting a limpia, doing a baño (see page 155), or using your limpia soap more regularly (see pages 152–54), or consider doing the lemon barrida mentioned in chapter five (see pages 158–59).

When choosing a candle for a velación, use whatever candle you feel guided to use, and if you are unsure which one you should use, consider asking for help from a saint or divine energy that calls to you. Here are some suggestions:

CANDLES HONORING DIVINE BEINGS

DIVINE BEING	MEANING
San Antonio (St. Anthony)	love
Buddha	petition where divine help is needed
Changó	good luck
Santa Clara	good fortune
Divina Providencia (Divine Providence)	prosperity
Santa Elena	discover the truth
St. Francis of Assisi	better understanding and peace
Ángel de la Guarda (Guardian Angel)	help looking over you and family members
Infant Jesus of Atocha	petition for help in any situation
San Juan Soldado	safe travels
San Judas Tadeo (St. Jude Thaddeus)	a miracle
Kuan Yin	help stop family quarrels, encourage compassion
St. Lazarus	guide in a new beginning
Santa Lucia	see with clarity
Lucky Buddha	good luck
Mano Poderosa	to help with work and business matters

DIVINE BEING	MEANING
Santa Marta	gain strength
San Martín de Porres	petition for financial needs
Archangel Michael	clear any type of negative energies
Our Lady of Grace	love
Our Lady of Guadalupe (Virgen de Guadalupe)	help stop family quarrels, encourage compassion
Our Lady of the Immaculate Conception	fertility and health
Our Lady of the Miraculous Medal	break bad habits
San Ramón	business prosperity
Archangel Raphael	healing, illumined vision
Sagrado Corazón de Jesús (Sacred Heart of Jesus)	petition where divine help is needed
Siete Potencias	get rid of bad luck
San Simón	have more financial abundance
Santa Teresa	increase the power of a magical petition
Yemaya	love

As for the color of the candles, here are some meanings:

THE COLORS OF CANDLES

COLOR	MEANING
White	all-purpose, purify a situation, and garner divine help
Blue	serenity and tranquility
Red	health and power
Pink	goodwill
Green	remove a harmful or a negative influence
Purple	repel dense energies
Black	bring closure to something or for magic

Divination Tools and Florida Water

The sacred items we place on our ancestral altars, our ancestors' homes, can definitely become infused with their soul energies, and they can intervene in our lives by guiding us through divination work. Divination items can include many different items, such as tarot cards, items for casting lots or sortilege—cacao beans, corn, legumes, shells—a puro (cigar), crystals, or other items used for scrying and understanding the probability of an outcome, and your own personalized Florida water.

Before placing these items on your ancestral altar, cleanse them by gently placing them over the orange part of the flames of a white fire limpia (see pages 38–39 for how to create a white fire limpia), smudging them with a bundle of herbs, spraying them with storebought or homemade Florida water, or blowing copal on them with a feather or feather fan. After cleansing them, introduce them to the ancestral altar, and invite your ancestor to infuse their soul energy into these sacred items.

I find that when using my own homemade Florida water that I had left on one of my ancestral altars to cleanse my hands before divination work, especially if it involves sortilege or picking cards from some kind of tarot deck, the reading of the cards is absolutely uncanny and spot on. I always thank the ancestors for guiding the divination work and providing us with their messages.

First are a few essentials: For a general all-purpose cleansing Florida water, use dry or fresh herbs, flowers, citrus peels, or spices that are aromatic. Good-smelling things are associated with good fortune and are believed to be the stuff our ancestors are made of. You also don't have to use all the items listed here: herbs, flowers, fresh citrus peels, and spices—but it is ideal to at least use a flower or herbs that grow flowers for traditional Florida water. If your Florida water is for all-purpose cleanses, include plants and fruits that purify, change misfortunes to great fortune, strengthen the energy bodies (a.k.a. protection), and encourage abundance. Vodka is another ingredient in Florida water. Some people will swear by really expensive vodka, but in my personal experience any vodka works. What makes it strong is the process, intention, and the plants and fruits that go into it.

Spiritual and Magical Properties of Plants and Fruit

Please adjust the amounts to what you feel called to use and have in your possession. Optimally, you would want a total of two full cups of fresh herbs or one cup of dried herbs, flowers, fresh citrus peels, and spices.

HERBS
(all provide overall purification)

HERB	ACTION	ATTRACTS	REPELS	STRENGTHENS
Rosemary	grounds	love	negativity	ancestral connections
Rue	clears	prosperity	negativity	energy fields
Basil	opens up pathways	abundance	negativity	mental clarity
Lemongrass	aids mental and emotional balance	clarity	depression	energy fields

FLOWERS

FLOWER	ACTION	ATTRACTS	REPELS	STRENGTHENS
Jasmine	induces prophetic dreams	abundance	self-doubt	ancestral connections
Cempazúchitl (Aztec marigold)	enhances divinatory work	success	misunderstanding and disharmony	ancestral connections
Roses	purifies	love (particularly red)	misunderstanding and disharmony	heart, love
Lavender	releases shame	creativity	anxiety	mental and emotional balance

SPICES
(use a tablespoon of one or more)

SPICE	ACTION	ATTRACTS	REPELS	STRENGTHENS
Allspice berries	abundance	great fortune	negativity and anger	energy
Cloves	clarifies the mind	positivity, good energy	accidents	energy fields
Cinnamon	opens pathways	financial abundance	blocks	divinatory work
Anise	enhances intuitive awareness	great fortune	sadness of the heart	energy fields

FRESH CITRUS PEELS
(use a peel of one fruit or more)

FRUIT	ACTION	ATTRACTS	REPELS	STRENGTHENS
Lemon	purifies	love	illnesses	energy
Orange	enhances magic	prosperity	depression	positivity
Grapefruit	enhances divinatory work	prosperity	scarcity	energy
Tangerine	enhances magic	closure	negative energy	energy fields

Below is one of my favorite recipes to make Florida water that is incredibly versatile and easy to make, and of course you can always buy Florida water at your local or online metaphysical store or in the ethnic section of most mainstream drug stores.

Making Florida Water

1. For the fresh plants, you want to squeeze them as you are washing them to get their natural oils out and compress their volume.
2. Place the fresh or dry plants (herbs, flowers, or spices) with 2½ cups of vodka in a pot. Put it on a low heat for 10 minutes. Put a lid on it so the vodka can reduce. Gently stir and make sure that everything has been covered with vodka.

3. After the 10 minutes, place the fresh plants—and if you are using citrus peels, those as well—in the pot. Keep it at a low heat for 45 additional minutes. Put a lid on it so the vodka can continue to reduce. Gently stir and make sure that everything has been covered with vodka.
4. Strain the contents with a wire mesh strainer, let them cool, and place your Florida water in a clean bottle.
5. Place the bottle on your ancestral altar or somewhere special.

Use this Florida water to cleanse your hands before doing divination work to ask your ancestors for guidance, aid, and intervention. If possible, leave this Florida water on your ancestral altar.

Gazing Rituals

Another way to have our ancestors continue their rebirth, intervention, and guidance is through gazing rituals. Place a candle, mirror, or their picture on your ancestral altar, and invite them to bless and infuse their soul energy into these sacred items. As for the candle, you can use any candle, and ideally it should be one where you can see the flame of the candle unhindered, so you can meditate and gaze into it.

Mirrors were and are still believed to be portals to the nonordinary realms. Traditionally, our Mesoamerican ancestors used obsidian, turquoise, and pyrite mirrors to engage in gazing rituals to obtain guidance from their ancestors, animal guides, deities, and other supernatural beings.

Performing a Gazing Ritual

Cleanse the space with a smudge herb bundle, white fire limpia (see pages 38–39), or your preferred way of cleansing spaces before engaging in this gazing ritual. Thereafter, it is ideal to offer copal or some pleasant-smelling resin or incense. I love copal because it cleanses spaces and inspires our ancestors to join us in this sacred space.

Dim the lights in the room for a relaxed ambience and so you can begin to see the subtle energies conveyed through these sacred items. Allow yourself to go into a trance meditative state by taking slow, intentional breaths, inhaling through the nose and exhaling out the mouth or nose, whichever feels more comfortable. Close your eyes and set the intention that your ancestor's messages will be relayed to you in this gazing ritual.

If you are using a mirror or candle, gently open your eyes one-tenth of the way and softly gaze into the mirror or the flame of the candle. If you are using a picture, look into the eyes of your ancestor. The eyes are also portals and can invoke the presence of your ancestor. Let yourself engage in a soft focus on any question you may have and thank your ancestor for their guidance. Continue this gazing ritual for at least fifteen minutes. Before closing the ritual, thank your ancestor once again for their guidance and ideal and graceful intervention.

Thereafter, very gently turn up the lights, and take five minutes to journal what came forward for you. Please try to avoid censoring the information. Reflect on how you felt during the gazing ritual. Did you get any visuals? Was or is there a sense of knowingness about something? If so, what? Did you hear any messages? It is helpful to pay attention to how energetic messages become known to us, so we become more cognizant when they happen outside of these intentional spaces. Please know that your ancestor will guide you as the days and weeks unfold, providing you with ideal guidance and intervention. The more you engage in ceremonial gazing, the stronger the connection becomes.

Soul Retrieval and Working with Our Ancestors in the North

Soul retrieval work* involves welcoming soul pieces of ourselves that left due to traumas we experienced in our present or past lives. Some telltale signs of soul losses typically include: recurrent difficult patterns, physical ailments, depression, insomnia, and other misfortunes. Soul pieces that have not returned, or have left once again, have done so typically because the person is engaging in or allowing some kind of analogous circumstances that caused the soul loss in the first place. The lost soul pieces can usually be found in the nonordinary realms. Because going

---

*I cover soul retrieval work in greater lengths in my second book, *Curanderismo Soul Retrieval.*

through the processes of soul retrieval requires strength, patience, self-love, and lots of compassion, it is incredibly helpful to work with the sacred energies of the cardinal space. The cardinal spaces are believed to be entities in their own right, associated with divine wisdom, sacred gifts, patrons, colors, World Trees, deities, day signs, year signs, mountains, and animals, and also emit their own soul energies, which can be incredibly helpful for soul retrieval work.

Because every cardinal space has its own axis mundi or World Tree, we can go to the North and ask our ancestors to help guide us through any one of the nonordinary realms, where our soul pieces may be residing in (see pages 29–37 to read about the nonordinary realms). If you feel like you may have experienced a soul loss and would love to receive soul energy both from the North and your ancestor to give you strength and whatever else you may need to keep you going and motivated, do so through a cacao ceremony.

Cacao Atole Ceremony

For this ceremony, you will need the following (Recipe is for one person.):

- 2 tablespoons of organic cornmeal
- 3 tablespoons of organic cacao powder
- 2 cinnamon sticks
- 1 teaspoon of vanilla extract
- honey (adjust per tastebuds)
- 2 cups of water

Place the organic cornmeal and the organic cacao powder that you will be using for your ceremony on your ancestral altar for a full moon cycle, starting one full moon to the next one. Offer copal or incense to the cacao and corn and invite your ancestor to infuse their soul energy into them.

At the end of the full moon cycle, engage in the cacao ceremony. Place 1 to 2 cinnamon sticks in a pot with 2 cups of water. Once it boils, lower it to a simmer and include the cornmeal. Once the cornmeal gets puffy, add honey, cacao, and vanilla extract. Gently stir these items in the pot until the honey completely melts. Let it cool as needed.

Cleanse the space where you will be engaging in the cacao ceremony with an herbal smudge stick, white fire limpia (see pages 38–39) explaining how to do white fire limpia), or your preferred way of cleansing spaces. Call in the North with a prayer and include sacred items, like a shell, fossil, flowers, instrument, tobacco, or pipe that you feel embodies ancestral medicine and wisdom. Invite your ancestor to join you in the ceremony and give you soul energy with this sacred brew. Before taking a drink honor the spirit of everything that was used to make this sacred brew and say a prayer of gratitude. Play loving medicine music and accept your ancestor's soul energy into you.

When closing thank your ancestor and your relations for giving you strength on your path of healing, self-awareness, and discovery.

CLAUDIA IS BLESSED WITH ANCESTRAL SOUL ENERGY AND HER FREEDOM

Claudia first came to me incredibly depressed, depleted, and desperate. She and her two children had recently moved in with her mother. She was in the process of initiating a divorce with her then husband. According to Claudia, her husband was a complete narcissist who constantly badmouthed and diminished her self-esteem. He was fifteen years older than she was and owned a successful landscaping company. The only activity that he allowed Claudia to engage in outside of her "obligations" as a wife and mother was going to the gym, so she could keep herself presentable for him.

Once their children began going to elementary school, Claudia wanted to work or perhaps go to school. She was feeling restless and wanted more from life. She expressed this to her husband. He became more aggressive in verbally abusing Claudia. Claudia admitted to me that when she first met her husband, it was exciting to be courted by someone who lavished and spoiled her with gifts and expensive dinners. She loved the attention. The courting began to dwindle during the first couple years of marriage. After she became a mother with their son, the courting came to an abrupt stop and became worse after the birth of their daughter. She had hoped that this would change after their children had gotten older, but he saw Claudia's request for romance as childish and selfish.

After continuous verbal and psychological abuse and cursing at her, she finally left with their children, moved in with her mother, and told him that she would be filing for divorce. But she left with very low self-esteem and was incredibly depressed. He told her that he would make sure that she would not get a penny from him nor would he agree to the divorce.

When Claudia described her faith and family relationships, her energy lightened and expanded when talking about her memories of her grandmother. Claudia's grandmother, who had lived with them throughout Claudia's life, had passed away when she was thirteen years old. Her grandmother was her best friend and advocate. She also picked her up and took her to school and extracurricular school activities for the first eleven years of her life. Anytime Claudia wanted to take part in an activity, her grandmother petitioned on her behalf. She also went to the school to complain to the principal and teacher after Claudia had been bullied in class. Her mother and father were in a toxic marriage and her grandmother was her lifeline to happiness and stability. Right before she turned twelve, her grandmother was diagnosed with late-stages endometrial cancer and passed a year and a half later. Her grandmother's passing was devastating for Claudia. She admitted to me that she still felt a deep sadness and loss by her passing.

I asked her to tell me how she honors her grandmother's memory. She said that she took flowers to her grave on holidays and her birthday. Claudia told me that she always felt her grandmother watching over her throughout her teenage years and young adult life. But her presence became weaker as she chose to stay married to her abusive husband. Claudia used to always have a picture of her grandmother on her nightstand. But when she moved in with her husband, he chastised her for keeping the picture next to her bed. After almost two years of moving in together, he moved the picture to a table in the living room hallway, which became hidden and buried by their other family pictures.

I asked Claudia if she wanted to invite her grandmother as an ancestor who would guide and intervene on her behalf. I explained some of the understandings of our Mesoamerican ancestors with regard to strengthening the soul energy of our ancestors, so they may be reborn, revitalized, and continue their existences in many different ways. I also showed her images of the Berlin Vase and focused on the images of the ancestor being reborn as cacao trees, their solar apotheosis, and cosmic renewal. I then facilitated a journey to guide her to connect with her grandmother, and offered Claudia and her grandmother healing from traumas, nonserving contracts, any generational cursing or ancestral cursing, and balancing of wrongdoings (see pages 144–52 in chapter 5). Our I Am divine presence always accepts what is ideal for us, and both Claudia and her grandmother accepted these healing gifts. Then, we invited Claudia's grandmother to be Claudia's ancestor and guide and intervene on her behalf, strengthening their energetic heart connection. After the session, Claudia felt an immediate shift and was ready to move forward with her divorce. I asked Claudia to create an ancestral altar for her grandmother, Ofelia, by doing a single seven-day candle velación, placing it over a petition asking for an ideal expeditious divorce and for an ideal outcome, and leaving it lit on the altar.

When Claudia came back to see me for her next session, she told me that her then husband was exhibiting a wide range of responses and reactions to her. For the first month since she had moved out, he refused to help her in any way—whether with money or picking up their children from school or other extracurricular activities. Claudia had begun working at her father's office as a secretary, and she needed a little help with their children. He refused to help in any way. Yet he repeatedly accused her of taking their children from him.

By this time, she had hired a family law attorney and had served her then husband with the divorce papers. She told me that she did indeed create an altar with pictures of Ofelia, her rosary, an idol of Our Lady of Guadalupe, a medallion of San Miguel, and a miniature rose bush. She also placed a glass of water for her and on Saturdays gave Ofelia her favorite pastries. She had also done her velación as I requested.

After the velación, her husband offered to give her a few hundred dollars to pay for their son's soccer shoes and for their daughter's gymnastic gear. He also offered to pick up their children and take them for a weekend. The glass from the velación, however, turned almost black. When she asked for more money, shortly after the velación and minor improvements, he refused and demanded that she come home with their children. I provided her with a limpia and instructed her to continue doing velaciones on her altar.

At our next session, she was a very different person. She laughed and told me that she was addicted to lighting candles because she noticed that every time she did so, her husband became much more reasonable. I had told her that velaciones always clear energy. When the glass turns black, it is energy that has been cleared, and the darkness and soot indicate we have to keep them up. She felt that for the first time in a long time there was hope out of an unhappy marriage, and she began working on her self-confidence, self-love, and self-worth. She was hopeful but also nervous about their first court date coming up. In the trance journey I helped facilitate, we worked with her grandmother Ofelia and thanked her for intervening to ensure an ideal expeditious divorce and an ideal outcome.

I felt Claudia's energy change drastically in this session and had a strong feeling her next velación would not be black. I asked her if she was ready to facilitate Ofelia's existence/soul energies in more ways and continue inviting her in her life as an ancestor. Claudia became incredibly excited and asked if she could do so by burning and burying the petition she wrote and placing a rose bush over it. She remembered the image of the Berlin Vase I showed her in our first session. Ofelia had an extensive rose garden and had loved it, especially her red roses. Sadly, they all died from a fungus a year after Ofelia died. I asked her to wait to burn and bury the ashes of the petition until after a glass from her single candle velación was no longer black, and to do so on the next full moon.

At our next session, Claudia came back even happier and full of hope and excitement. She informed me that the glass from her last velación was clear. She also burned the petition and buried the ashes on the morning of the new moon, and placed a beautiful red rose bush on top. On the day of their court appearance, however, her then husband had an emergency at work and did not appear. When Claudia came home that day, her mother informed Claudia that her mother's German shepherd slightly toppled the red rose bush she had recently planted. She also admitted to me that she did not ask her mother for permission to bury the red roses in honor of her grandmother and to encourage the continuance and rebirth of her soul energies. Although her mother loved her mother-in-law, she did not tell her mother the full extent of what she was doing. I recommended that this was important as this was not her home, and her mother's dog likely sensed what she was doing and felt this was a sort of energetic trespass. I reminded her that animals are very intuitive. She told me that she would ask for consent from her mother, invite her mother to say a few words, and would also request a small fence be placed around the rosebush.

A few weeks after this session, she emailed me thrilled, notifying me that her husband signed the divorce papers, agreed to a reasonable split of the community property assets, and was paying for spousal and child support. She received majority custody due to her husband's busy work schedule. She successfully planted her rose bush and felt an even stronger connection with her grandmother. Currently, Claudia is the office manager at her father's business and just closed escrow on a small house, where she will be living with her children.

CHAPTER 5

Working with Deified Ancestral Sacred Energies for Healing Purposes

Healing my ancestral lineages has been an incredibly critical aspect of my healing journey. While I may call all of my deceased blood family members "ancestors," as I mentioned earlier, there are only two blood family ancestors I invoke to hold space for me when I am doing my own personal healing work. The other ancestors I invoke are cultural and vocational ancestors. I sometimes call this my ancestral entourage. Together with my ancestral entourage we also offer healing for my blood ancestral lineage and sometimes my clients. Getting to know my ancestral entourage has taken place through the numerous ancestral veneration rites I have mentioned throughout this book, and especially working with an ancestral bundle that went everywhere that was special to me for over two decades.

In 1999, I purchased my first ancestral bundle from a store in Playa del Carmen and began doing my own ancestral veneration and healing work. I took my ancestral bundle everywhere sacred and special I went, which included different kinds of ceremonies, trips to sacred sites, placing it over my pillow to engage in dreamwork with my ancestors, or letting it rest and recharge on my ancestral altar. I created my first ancestral altar a year after purchasing it. My Maya ancestors definitely guided me toward this bundle.

Back in 1999, Playa del Carmen was a gorgeous and relatively low-key town. Its downtown shops consisted of one main street. I went into town to purchase herbs for that night's full moon *temezcal* (sweat-bath ceremony). I had a little time before the ceremony and walked into a store that had extraordinary hide bundles, instruments, resins, urns, and other sacred items. My ancestral bundle caught my eye with its brilliantly bold-colored glyphs of the Maya Calendar Round. Somehow, I began remembering what the glyphs meant and began to share what I was seeing with the Maya lady that owned the shop. She was standing next to me as I admired its beauty. At that time, I had not yet studied these glyphs in my waking state. I nervously asked her how much it was. I did not come prepared to shop and had less than ten dollars on me. She asked me how much I had. I pulled out everything I had. She smiled and said it was mine. That evening I took my bundle into the temezcal, and after coming out of the temezcal, I laid my head on it and gazed into the full moon. The next day I went back to the store to repay the lady the difference for the bundle. The odd thing was that I was unable to find the store again. I spent a few hours looking for the store and asking people about it but was unable to find it, despite walking up and down the street I had been on the day before. My ancestors orchestrated that connection and this ancestral bundle has since remained very dear to me.

Anytime I need guidance about anything, I place this ancestral bundle on my pillow and thank my ancestors for guiding me in my dreams. From 2017 through 2019, I slept with it more regularly, approximately once a week. I needed guidance from my ancestors about the purchase of our ideal home. We intended to purchase a new home in 2016, but home prices in Los Angeles suddenly spiked. My husband and I wanted a larger-sized property so we could hold classes and workshops at our place, engage in urban farming, be close to nature and the mountains, and still be close to Los Angeles.

When we told real estate agents what we were looking for and our price range, they told us finding something like this was highly unlikely. Yet my ancestors told me in my dreams to be patient and continue upgrading our current home. Every week we searched all available real estate websites four to five times a week for our dream home. One Sunday morning, I woke up and told my husband that our home was ready for us. That night, my ancestors made this vision very clear to me in a dream. That morning we found a home that matched what we were looking for. We went to see it that day, fell in love with it, and made an offer on it the next day. Although we exposed ourselves to two potential mortgages, I knew my ancestors were guiding its purchase. We sold our current home in less than two weeks and only had two weeks of two mortgages. We moved into our new home in Tujunga the next month. I know the strong relationship I have developed with my ancestors through veneration rites and healing work has strengthened their soul energies, which allows them to intervene in my life. I see my ancestors as pure, loving, wise, divine energy.

Ancient Mesoamerican ancestors were often worshipped as divine beings who could infuse their deified energies into sacred items, become deified ancestors or deities themselves—expressions of the same soul-animating energies—and, especially in the cases of ancestral rulers, undergo an apotheosis and become aspects or incarnations of the Sun or Maize Deity.[1] Ancestral veneration ceremonies enabled both the strengthening or deification of their soul energies and the infusion of their soul energies into their portraits, figurines, ancestral bundles, clothes, jewelry, and other personal belongings. These infused items were often worshipped, consulted, and treated as the ancestor themself. The ancestors they chose to venerate in such a manner could then play more significant roles in their lives, especially regarding guiding, aiding, healing, and intervening on their heir's behalf.

After examining the ancient Mesoamerican deification of ancestors, how ancestors and deities were in some cases expressions of each other, and the sacred items that were infused with their soul energies, I will delve into vivifying our ancestral bundles and working with our chosen ancestors for healing purposes. The healing will include working with our chosen ancestors to offer clearing of curses and the balancing of wrongdoings to our chosen ancestors and family. We also cover other curanderismo limpia rites that can support us by clearing and revitalizing our energies and strengthening the potency of our beautiful ofrendas to our ancestors, ourselves, and family. I also share how the ancestor of one of my clients infused her with his soul energy to leave her toxic home environment.

DEIFIED ANCESTORS AND DEITIES AND EXPRESSIONS OF EACH OTHER

The fascinating and multilayered understandings of ancestors and deities as beings comprised of the same sacred energy, mirroring each other, becoming aspects of one another, and incarnating as one another can be seen in Maya artwork, codices, and mythologies. The four incised bones from Hasaw Ka'an K'awiil's Burial 116 at Tikal depict the paddler gods and other cosmic beings, likely facilitating the cosmic journey this ancestral ruler would be playing or one of his ancestors played. The Maya paddler gods, who get their name from their role paddling a dugout canoe, offered a cosmic transportation service for the recently deceased or those about to enter or reenter the world of the living.[2] The Maya paddler gods facilitated a kind of recycling of sacred soul energies and the transference of it in different forms.

Sacred artwork as a means of ancestral veneration often commemorated and facilitated the ancestor's cosmic apotheosis and also provided the means of their deification, such as with Pakal's sarcophagus lid, which functioned as a container for his remains and a vehicle for his rebirth.[3] At the Temple of the Inscriptions, also at Palenque, the iconography identifies Pakal's birth and accession as the K'atun ending 9.9.0.0.0.* His

---

*The Maya observed calendrical rites associated with both the Long Count calendar and the Calendar Round. The Long Count is a remarkably sophisticated and complex calendric system that incorporated massive periods of time from the starting point of this calendar, September 8, 3114 BCE. Typically, the largest unit was the bak'tun (approximately 400 years), the next was the k'atun (approximately twenty years), then the tun (360 days), then the winal (20 days), and finally the k'in (a single day). Long Count dates are typically presented with the bak'tun first and the k'in position at the end, followed by the Calendar Round.[6]

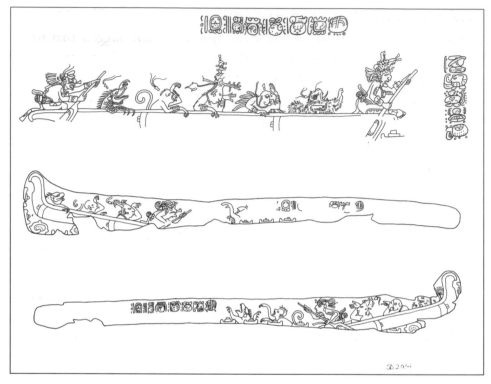

Fig. 5.1 Three inscribed bones from Tikal Burial 116 show paddler
deities in a canoe bearing a maize god and supernatural,
anthropomorphic iguana, spider monkey, parrot, and dog.
Courtesy of Ancient Americas at LACMA. SD-2014.
Drawing by Linda Schele. Copyright © David Schele.

accession is immediately thereafter linked to a remote deity who "became
a lord" 1,247,654 years beforehand. Interestingly, there is another date
commemorating Pakal's accession 4,000 years in the future.[4] Pakal as
a deified ancestor was connected with past deities, his royal ancestors,
and could affect the distant future. The well-preserved hieroglyphs at
Temple XIX at Palenque also denote a possible rebirth of creator deity,
GI (referring to "God One"), one of Palenque's principal triad gods, on
the same day of the seating of ancestral ruler K'inich Ahkal Mo' Nahb.
On the day of the ruler's accession, he is depicted as wearing distinctive
emblems associated with deity GI, such as a small heron grasping a fish in
its beak. His accession took place on 9 *Ik*, which was also the mythologi-

cal date of the enthronement of GI. They chose the date of the ancestral ruler's accession to evoke cosmological significance and suggest that he was also made of the same sacred soul energies as the gods.[5]

The artwork of the postclassic Mixtec, the Codex Zouche-Nuttal, depicts a supernatural ancestor becoming a human being. The opening pages depict the rain god pouring water from a handled jug over Lord 8 Wind. Lord 8 Wind is being baptized by the rain god. Lord 8 Wind is thereafter transformed into a full human, who is able to marry and have children.[7]

The sixteenth-century ethnohistoric records of the central Mexicans identify the tutelary deity of the Mexica, Huitzilopochtli, and his mother, Coatlique, as deities and supernatural human ancestors. They were deities in the mundane Middleworld, and yet, could be seen by humans as supernatural human ancestors in a sacred parallel Middleworld dimension. The Florentine Codex notes that the origin of Huitzilopochtli was at Coatepec Hill, near Tula, where he lived with his mother and sister, Coyolxauhqui.[8] In the codex, Huitzilopochtli is identified as a "common man, a sorcerer."[9]

During Motecuhzoma II's reign, the second-to-last Mexica ruler, he sought the origin of his ancestors at Chicomoztoc, the Seven Caves. He believed that Coatlique was still alive, so he sent sixty wizards, sorcerers, and magicians to find her. It was said that Coatlique still lived in leisure, never became weary or old, and didn't lack for anything.[10] They left, and when they reached the Coatepec hill, they asked to see the home of their ancestors. They were taken to the shores of a large lake and saw strangers speaking the same language. They told them they sought Coatlique and Chicomoztoc, the Seven Caves, and had gifts for her. They took the Mexica across the lake to the hill of Colhuacan. The Mexica were unable to climb this hill, so an ancestor brought the items and the men up the hill. Coatlique, a woman of great age, appeared, and she told them that she had been waiting for her son, weeping for him to return.[11] When the sorcerers who had survived the arduous journey returned, they confirmed that all the ancestors who had stayed there were alive.[12]

Ancestor Depictions and Their Deification

Ancestral veneration rites could enliven items—clothes, accoutrements, staffs, silverware, their portraits—that were created to commemorate the ancestor's passing or used by them while they were alive. They were in turn worshipped and people treated these sacred items as the ancestor. The early and mid-Classic Maya often depicted their ancestors as floating heads. Solar, lunar, and stellar cartouches are widely associated with ancestor spirits in Maya art, especially on monuments from the Yaxchilan kingdom.[13] The upper registers of Yaxchilan stelae, the ancestor cartouches, and heads of ancestors are associated with both the Sun and the Moon and depict their apotheosis and road into these celestial realms.[14]

The carved stone portraits of the Mexica rulers at Chapultepec were worshipped and honored as the royal ancestors themselves. Chapultepec was important to the Mexica because it was the place where they settled, chose their very first ruler, and made the first sacrifice to the deities.[15] Itzcoatl ordered his image and those of his ancestors be carved in stone there for an everlasting memorial.[16] The subsequent rulers also commissioned their images to be carved on the stones. The Mexica made ritual offerings to these images and worshipped them as the ancestor ruler.[17]

Figurines of ancestors made of wood, clay, stone, or precious jewels were also regarded as embodying aspects of the ancestor's soul energies and could be used to communicate with the ancestors.[18] Ancestral figurines date back to Teotihuacán.[19] The Zapotec of Oaxaca placed pottery figurines inside ancestral tombs, in their antechambers, or in front of the tomb door. Some caches of small figurines seem to have been buried as a group to preserve their arrangement as a scene.[20] One scene below the south half wall of the inner room, Feature 96, likely depicts the metamorphosis of a royal ancestor becoming a cloud deity in contact with lightning.[21] Ancestral lightning figurines may have served several functions, including to protect or guard the tomb, to mediate the flow of communications between the deceased in the tomb and their descendants in the residence above, to honor deceased ancestors, and to rekindle memories of the ancestors on the anniver-

SD-2045

Fig. 5.2. A Maya Classic-period depiction of a disembodied
head of an ancestor. Tikal, Stela 29.
Courtesy of Ancient Americas at LACMA. SD-2045.
Drawing by Linda Schele. Copyright © David Schele.

saries of their deaths.[22] Some Zapotec figurine vessels depict ancestors as either metamorphosizing into lightning deities or wearing the masks of supernatural beings.[23]

Among the sixteenth-century Yucatec Maya the practice of creating wooden ancestor figurines for placement in shrines and other ritual locations was widespread. These wooden figurines were kept in homes alongside figurines of other important ancestors. On feast days, the figurines were given offerings of food and celebrated as the ancestors themselves. These ancestral figurines were loved by later generations and were kept as heirlooms.[24] Along with offerings of food and drink, they burned incense before them.[25]

Ancestral figurines were also honored and given offerings on the Mexica solar months of Toxcatl, Xocotl Uetzi, Tepeilhuitl, and likely in many other private and familial ceremonies. Mexica rulers were also often cremated with their figurines.[26] The ancestral wooden figurines that were placed on the earthen vessel or box that contained the ancestor's ashes, hair, and the chalchíhuitl (green stone that symbolized the ancestor's heart) were provided offerings at the place where the box was buried.[27]

The veneration and honoring of ancestral bundles, and the bundling of ancestral remains—the corpse, defleshed bones, or ashes—in some material, were also common practices throughout Mesoamerica. They were buried, curated, displayed on altars, manipulated in rituals, consulted, and worshiped.[28] Ancestral bundles destined for cremation are often seen in the art of Teotihuacán and the later Mixtec and Mexica.[29] The Mexica viewed ancestral bundles as a deified source that gave them success in their political power and guarded them well.[30] Ideologically, ancestral bundling relates to a long and complex history of bundling spiritually potent objects, in this case the spiritually charged bones, ashes, or charged items of the ancestors, which needed to be cared for and protected.[31]

In myths of origin, ancestral bundles were often given by deities, primordial ancestors, or founding patriarchs, often at the beginning of new calendrical cycles. They were also carried in pilgrimages as symbols of group identity and charters for the predestined ascendancy of ethnic groups and their lineages.[32] In codices and artwork, ancestral bundles were sometimes depicted with speech scrolls, suggesting that they were guiding their heirs.

In Teotihuacán, flexed corpse bundling—bundled corpses interred in an upright position—was very common.[33] There is also archaeological evidence for the burning of ancestral bundles, which were placed in a burning burial pit at Teotihuacán.[34]

Pl. XVII

Fig. 5.3. Depicts the practice of carving of ancestor heads
for ancestral veneration rites.
Courtesy of Ancient Americas at LACMA. Codex Madrid, 96d.

Ancestral bundles were a recurrent motif of Classic-period iconography in the Maya lowlands, and were glyphic expressions for the inheritance of political power and accession to office. Other bundles are known to have contained bloodletting paraphernalia used to invoke ancestors.[35] The bundling of ancestors is also apparent on the Berlin Vase and Stela 40 from Piedras Negras.[36] Additionally, ancestral bundles have been found at the tombs of Maya Classic-period Calakmul. Tomb 1 of Structure 15 contained a woman who had been wrapped in three layers of textile that was hardened by resin, perhaps rubber or chicle.[37] In some instances, ancestral bundles were carried into battle as a source of power and fortitude and, like stela, were captured in warfare.[38]

Mixtec codices also depict ancestral bundles being delivered from the Upperworld by deities or their priests. They also appear in the context of polity founding and in fire-drilling rituals that symbolized the annexation of conquered polities.[39] Mixtec ancestral bundles were consulted by oracular priests acting as mediums for guidance on political questions, war, marriage, and everyday matters.[40]

Page 21 of the Codex Zouche-Nuttal shows a war conducted by Lady 9 Grass and Lord 9 Wind immediately followed by the burning of ancestral bundles of two rival Mixtec lords. These bundles were captured in war and burned to destroy the ancestors, which were apparently believed to be the powerbase of rival lineages.[41] Codex Seldan 1064:9-I depicts incensing ceremonies occurring in shrines and before ancestral bundles.[42]

INTEGRATING ANCIENT MESOAMERICAN WISDOM

Ancestral Bundles, Healing, and Limpia Rites

The soul energies of the ancestors of the ancient Mesoamericans were believed to be strengthened through their various ancestral veneration rites. Ancestors were often treated as divine beings whose soul energies could be continued, renewed, and rebirthed in many ways and could exist in different nonordinary realms and levels. These stronger and deified ancestors were treated as being pivotal to not just the identity of communities, but also to their source of power and fortune, as they could intervene, aid, guide, and heal their heirs with greater expediency and effectiveness.

Honoring our ancestors with the numerous ancestral veneration rites that have been discussed thus far can strengthen our ancestor's soul energies and, with their aid, can enable the potency of our healing to all of our other ancestors, ourselves, family members, and our family generations to come. Before I delve into ancestral healing and limpia rites that will support our processes of healing, I strongly recommend vivifying an ancestral bundle, through which you can have your ancestors join you in ceremonies, sweat lodges, dreamwork, meditations, hiking excursions, and trips to sacred sites through your bundle. If you feel providing healing to your ancestral lineages needs to be done first, then please do so. Having an ancestral entourage, however, that can help you hold space for your ancestral lineages, can be absolutely invaluable and incredibly powerful as you go deeper in your processes of healing and self-awareness. Taking our ancestral entourage with us to ceremonies, special events, and places, and having them engage in dreamwork with us, can definitely strengthen our relationship with them, and can be done via our ancestral bundles—and, of course, as was discussed on pages 67–70, by taking a sacred item from our ancestral altar with us when we need more of their strength, support, and intervention.

Ancestral Bundles

Ancestral bundles can serve as altar pieces where our sacred tools and other sacred items are placed, cleansed, and charged with the soul energies of our ancestors. They can also join us in transit and can be placed on our pillow for dreamwork practices. While ancestral bundles are precious cloths or hides, what is precious is absolutely subjective. A precious cloth can be a bandana, rebozo, or a cloth with a sacred mythological depiction—a creation scene, deity, or saint. Precious cloths or hides with sacred mythological depictions can be found at Mesoamerican sacred sites that have vendors. At Chichen Itza, for example, there are beautiful hides with scenes of the Maya World Tree, Calendar Round, Pakal's sarcophagus lid, and much more. Beautiful artwork on cloths of Huichol mythological creation scenes can also be found via an internet search. But, again, what is precious is completely up to you, and you can, of course, make anything precious with your intention and your vivification ritual.

When you decide on your ancestral bundle, please consider cleansing it in ways you like to be cleansed. You can cleanse it by:

- Carefully running a lit herbal smudge bundle over it
- Carefully running it over the top of the orange flames of a white fire limpia (refer to pages 38–39)
- Running a puro (a tobacco cigar) with a feather fan over the bundle
- Spraying your bundle with blessed water (Florida water, rose water, Moon water, or holy water) and saying a prayer over it
- Puffing in smoke from an herb or tobacco and blowing it on the bundle
- Saying a prayer, singing a medicine song, or chanting to the bundle

You can vivify your ancestral bundle with the soul energy of a specific ancestor, a group of cultural, vocational, blood ancestors, ancestors related to a sacred land, or your ancestors as a whole—work intuitively in this vivifying ritual. In vivifying our ancestral bundles with the soul energies of our ancestors, think of a cycle that is special to you. Just like humans and all of nature have cycles of coming to life and maturity, vivifying them should be done in cycles as well. Similar to the bundle, what is understood as a cycle of life is again subjective and ideally should be personalized to you. After all, your ancestral bundle and you are embodying the same or similar soul energy, so your cycles of life should coincide. These cycles can be a lunar cycle, your birthday (from the time you were born for a twenty-four-hour period), or a full day, week, or a month that is special to you.

Once you have chosen your cycle of vivification, choose the sacred items you will use to vivify your ancestral bundle. They can definitely be items that are on your ancestral altar and are special to you. Items that are special to us tend to carry our soul energies. It is tradition to vivify the bundle with the sacred energies and medicine of the cardinal spaces and nonordinary realms by using sacred items that represent and embody these sacred energies and the soul energies of our ancestors. (For ideas as far as what items to use, see pages 65–67 on cosmic spacing.) You would place these items on your bundle as shown.

PLACEMENT OF ITEMS WITHIN ANCESTRAL BUNDLE*

	North *Upperworld*	
West	Center *Middleworld*	East
	South *Underworld*	

*The Upperworld, Middleworld, and Underworld can also be conflated with the cardinal spacing positioning for the gifts of the cardinal spaces and nonordinary realms (see pages 66–67).

Keep in heart and mind that choosing these sacred items is an integral part of this ceremony, so leave a good amount of time to allow yourself to be guided and tune into what feels right for you to use to charge your ancestral bundle. Have these sacred items out, cleanse them (see above), and then invite your ancestors to infuse their soul energies into these items and onto your ancestral bundle during your chosen cycle of vivification. This ceremony can be as elaborate or simple as you are called for it to be. If possible after your ceremony, leave your sacred items on your sacred bundle for at least a day or longer. Continue to work intuitively as to how often you may need to give the ancestral bundle a limpia, and remember that giving our sacred items limpias is a way we show these items and our ancestors love. Let your ancestral bundle get revitalized on your altar. Again, work intuitively when doing so.

Healing Ourselves and Our Ancestral Lineages

Before I delve into ancestral healing, I must again stress that healing is generally not experienced in a linear manner. Sometimes we need to sit with a chosen ancestor and engage in different kinds of ancestral veneration rites before we embark on working with that ancestor for healing purposes. There may be other times we may sense that offering healing to an ancestor and ourselves should be our first step or our first set of steps. We may also perceive it is more in alignment to work fluidly, in that we may start by whatever feels right—strengthening our connection with a chosen ancestor through veneration rites or offering them healing, then continuing to strengthen our bonds for some time, and then continuing our healing journeys together, while intermittently engaging in ancestral veneration rites.

Reflecting back, for the two blood ancestors whom I work with as part of my ancestral entourage, I started by offering them the same healing gifts I received before I began more regular veneration rites to my growing ancestral entourage. Most of the cultural and vocational ancestors who have come forward for me took place through ancestral veneration rites, namely, by me making offerings to them and including them in my ancestral altar. Once we established what felt like an ancestral connection and relationship, I offered healing, clearing, and rescripting to them as I was guided. Inspired by my ancient Mesoamerican ancestors, I feel an intuitive combination of healing and veneration rites opens pathways for them to intervene, aid, guide, and heal myself, clients, other ancestors, and ancestral and familial lineages. Your journey, however, may be completely different or somewhat parallel to mine. Let yourself be called to what is needed, and flow with what feels in alignment with you.

Considerations for Offering Ancestral Healing

It is believed that the traumas our ancestors experienced, as well as the wrongdoings they may have perpetrated, are often played out or experienced by their heirs, particularly blood heirs. We may experience them as reoccurring patterns we personally experience and see in our family, similar to Beth's story of the women in her family being involved with unfaithful men. We may experience these ancestral traumas or wrongdoings as unexplained anxiety, stress, or depression triggered by certain people or circumstances.

During the first journey into your sacred heart to connect with your ancestor or strengthen the bond with your ancestor (see pages 37–44 for the explanation of sacred journey into heart), please consider offering the ancestor who has come forward any or all of the healing gifts discussed in the latter part of this chapter and any other healing gifts you feel they may need. These healing gifts will no doubt strengthen their soul energies and also strengthen your connection and bond with them.

If you believe a healing, clearing, balancing, or rescripting of ancestral traumas or wrongdoings may be needed, please take some time and space for yourself to reflect and prepare yourself with self-care and self-love before and after doing this work. Consider engaging in any of the following that day or the days before and after:

- Physical self-care such as yoga, qigong, and cardio. Consider staying away from meat. With very rare exceptions, meat industries in general are not very humane. Animals carry this trauma, and we in turn consume this energy. You want to avoid being weighed down energetically when doing this work.
- Mental self-care such as taking a nap that day or at least closing your eyes and resting or meditating for ten to twenty minutes.

- Emotional self-care such as watching or reading something uplifting and positive.
- Spiritual self-care such as repeating positive affirmations about yourself in the mirror.

It is also important to remember to avoid not getting attached to the ancestral stories of trauma that come up. Your role is to facilitate healing rather than continuing to replay the trauma(s) of our ancestors.

As exciting and beautiful as this work may be, please allow yourself to be graceful in the process of facilitating healing for yourself, the ancestors, and ancestral lineages, and refrain from rushing the process. Every time you connect with an issue and your ancestor or ancestral lineages, you begin to peel away at the layers of healing that may be needed for yourself, the ancestor, and ancestral lineages. We may work on a particular issue or trauma, and guess what? At another point in time you will have to revisit that same issue or trauma, as there may be another layer that needs your attention—often because you are now ready to work with that issue or trauma.

When we heal, clear, and rescript our prior traumas and those of our ancestors and ancestral lineages, this takes place on an energetic level that eventually seeps into our third-dimensional reality or causal physical realms. How fast it affects our physical realities and the lives of our family members depends on various factors, including: the scope of our intentions; how committed we are to doing our work of self-discovery, releasing, reconnection, and practicing healthy self-love; and the strength of our soul energies and our ancestor's soul energies, as well as our bond with one another. Remember that we strengthen the bond with our ancestors and our reciprocal soul energies with ancestral veneration rites and ancestral healing rites. Every time we engage in ancestral healing, we also have an opportunity to open up pathways to experience a more ideal life free of reliving or replaying ancestral traumas.

TYPES OF ANCESTRAL HEALING GIFTS

The healing gifts I discuss below are, of course, not all-encompassing, and should be tailored to what intuitively feels right for you. The recommended healing gifts should serve as possible points of reflection and consideration.

Scope of Ancestral Healing

There are many approaches to offering ancestral healing, and your approach largely depends on your scope and intention. It can be simply to offer healing to an ancestor or a lineage of ancestors from this lifetime. If you are just starting out doing this work, this is a beautiful place to start. The ancestral lineage can include women (grandmothers), men (grandfathers), LGBTQ+ ancestors generally, or a lineage that experienced a particular type of trauma. It can also include ancestors outside of your direct blood lineage, such as vocational or cultural ancestors or ancestors related to sacred lands. In these scenarios, you may want to consider developing a stronger connection with them first so you get a better sense of their stories and what kind of healing gifts may be in alignment for them.

Ancestral healing can also include offering healing gifts to ancestors from past lives and other quantum realities—parallel (intra/inter) dimensions. The important part is not to get in our head about these alternate scenarios, especially because our analytical mind often has a difficult time processing frameworks outside of the linear space-time continuum. Rather, stay in your sacred heart and intuitively tune into what is needed, and you can simply set the intention to offer healing to all of your ancestors (or a specific set of ancestors related to a specific issue) connected or associated with you from any other realities or spaces. It is enough to be aware that these other realities and possibilities exist. Integrate this awareness in your intention without having to know the exact details of why, who, where, when, or what.

If we can fathom, even for a glimpse, that there may be a reality or past life where our ancestors could have been the "transgressor/aggressor" or could have been on the receiving end of aggression, we can also continue to fine tune the arts and gifts of genuine compassion and understanding. This of course does not mean that we have to accept what was done as permissible or honor that ancestor as an ancestor we will be working with as part of our ancestral entourage and other healing practices; rather, it means we have the spiritual maturity to facilitate the healing, clearing, and rescripting for all of our ancestors. Keep in mind also that energetic ties, such as strong love or resentment, may keep groups of people connected to one another in previous, present, and subsequent lifetimes, so often you will be working with the same or similar group(s) of people and ancestors.

In offering healing to your ancestors, please consider that integral components of Mesoamerican cosmology involved the concepts of duality, equilibrium, and fluidity.[43] Duality was a dynamic principle that was constantly giving its impulse to ongoing causal change. The world was always in a state of flux, while at the same time continuously reestablishing and rebalancing itself. This balancing definitely included wrongdoings or trespasses committed against others. A critical goal was to maintain balance with all of our relations in a world that was constantly reestablishing itself.[44]

Before death, it was common to summon a *tlapouhqui,* a shaman of Tlazolteotl* skilled in the reading and interpretation of the sacred books, so that the dying person could confess all wrongdoings—a balancing or straightening of the heart, a *plática* "heart-straightening talk." If the confessor was a person of importance, the plática would take place at their home; if not, the person would go to the tlapouhqui on the day advised. The two would sit on new mats beside a fire. The tlapouhqui threw incense into the flames and invoked the deities while smoke

---

*Tlazolteotl, known as the Great Spinner and Weaver or the Filth Deity, was associated with sweeping limpia rites, fertility and childbirth, the Moon, menses, the steam bath, purification, sexuality, witchcraft, healing, and sexual misdeeds. She absolved sins, healed illnesses, and forgave.[45]

filled the air. The tlapouhqui would call out to the deities, letting them know of the confessor's request to have a plática. Then the tlapouhqui instructed the confessor to confess without restraint or shame.[46]

The confessor touched the earth with a finger, swore to do so, and told of their life at length, recounting wrongdoings. The person was supposed to tell all and conceal nothing. The tlapouhqui typically commanded the confessor to engage in penances, such as making restitution to persons harmed, engaging in fasts, and piercing the tongue. Once the penance had been completed, the confessor was absolved and all actions were balanced, and they could no longer be punished for previous wrongdoings.[47]

Petitioning for the balancing of wrongdoings, whether committed or experienced by our ancestors, is an opportunity for us to humbly petition that these wrongdoings be balanced, thereby providing opportunities for us to experience a more ideal life free of reliving or replaying these transgressions in any way. We are playing the role of the tlapouhqui in offering these gifts to our ancestors and ourselves, petitioning for and facilitating a balancing of various different types of wrongdoings. Please do keep in mind that we will likely need to learn whatever lessons need to be learned from the wrongdoings, especially if we committed them in this lifetime or other lifetimes. We can nonetheless ask that we learn these lessons with ideal ease and grace, and assuming our actions are in alignment with this, we can facilitate the rebalancing, avoiding unwanted patterns or illnesses in our lives.

Offering Ancestral Healing

When I am doing ancestral healing for my blood ancestral lineages, my ancestral entourage steps in and holds space with me. This entourage may also step in and help facilitate ancestral healing for my clients and their ancestors. My ancestral entourage are ancestors whom I have developed a deep connection with through diverse and ongoing ancestral veneration rites and involving them in my healing journeys for myself, them, other ancestors, and ancestral lineages. When it feels right, invite an ancestor to help to facilitate healing gifts for yourself, them, your other ancestors, or ancestral lineages.

Take some time to reflect on the scope—which ancestor or ancestors you will be offering the healing gifts to and the types of healing gifts you will be offering to them—before engaging in ancestral healing. And, of course, you can adjust the scope and intention if you feel a more expansive or narrow scope or intention is necessary when you are involved in your journey work.

I recommend embarking on the recommended journey into the sacred heart when engaging in ancestral healing (see pages 37–44). After stepping into your sacred heart, shine a light from your sacred heart and, if it feels appropriate, invite an ancestor or various guides to help you facilitate the ancestral healing. Tune in once again to your scope and intention.

Invite the ancestor or ancestral lineage into your sacred heart, the heart of God, the heart of love, the heart of oneness. You can ask them what they would like healing for or from or offer them these healing gifts instead. Because this facilitating of healing gifts is energy work, especially if you are starting out, I recommend taking it somewhat slowly. For example, start with clearing curses from a specific ancestral lineage. Once you become more familiar with the levels of energies required to facilitate this healing, are practicing disciplined self-care and self-love, are doing regular limpias for yourself, and knowing with greater certainty that you are the I Am divine presence with strong, humble conviction, you can begin working on quantum levels with significantly more grace.

After you have offered healing gifts, know that the I Am of any soul you are offering healing gifts to, dead or alive, always accepts what is ideal for them. The healing gifts will strengthen their soul energies and could facilitate a more graceful existence for them in the afterlife nonordinary realms and, as indicated, can help to make your path and generational heirs more graceful. Thank all of the ancestors and guides who may have joined you. Then exit from your sacred heart as explained on pages 42–44.

Clearing Curses

We typically know ancestral curses need to be cleared if there are unwanted and recurring patterns that have taken place in families (such as illness, poverty, infidelity, or problematic relationships). These sometimes affect only the men or women or the firstborn, or sometimes entire families are affected. In this context, curses include intentionally directed adverse magic, or when someone mentally and emotionally curses someone and their ancestral lineage out of anger. Once inside your sacred heart, when you feel it is in alignment to offer a clearing of curses, consider the scope of ancestral clearing.

Ask yourself questions to determine who the clearing is for.

- Are you included in the clearing? If so, state or set the intention, "In the name of my I Am presence I also offer this clearing to my I Am presence."
- Is the clearing for a particular ancestor or ancestral lineage? If so, state or set the intention, "In the name of my I Am presence I offer this clearing to (particular ancestor) or (ancestral lineage)."
- Is the clearing offered to your ancestors on a quantum level? If so, state, "In the name of my I Am presence, I offer this clearing to all of my ancestors related to or associated with my I Am presence everywhere I exist, have existed, or will exist and have been cursed in any way (or state what you believe the curse is related to)."

Next, consider the scope of your gifting, and use any or all of the gifts for clearing you feel in alignment with.

- "I offer the removal of any and all soul agreements to bring forward curses from any ancestral lines."
- "I offer the resolution of all curses from past life experiences or realities."

- "I offer the resolution of curses for where _____ (fill in who the clearing is for) may have cursed others in all lifetimes or realities."
- "I offer the dissolution of any harm cords and balancing of wrong-doings between the events and persons involved in the cursing. And that any lessons from any wrongdoings be learned with ideal ease and grace, please and thank you."

Balancing Wrongdoings

Ask yourself questions to determine who the balancing of wrongdoings is for.

- Are you included in the balancing of wrongdoings? If so, state or set the intention, "In the name of my I Am presence I offer this balancing of wrongdoings to my I Am presence."
- Is the balancing of wrongdoings for particular ancestor(s) or your ancestral lineage? If so, state or set the intention, "In the name of my I Am presence I offer the balancing of wrongdoings to (particular ancestor) or my (ancestral lineage)."
- Is the balancing of wrongdoings offered to your ancestors on a quantum level? If so, state "In the name of my I Am presence I offer the balancing of wrongdoings to all of my ancestors related or associated with my I Am everywhere I exist, have existed, or will exist."

And finally, close the questioning with a prayer, "I ask that any and all lessons that may still need to be learned from the wrongdoings be learned with ideal ease and grace, please and thank you."

Curanderismo Limpia Rites to Support Ancestral Healing

Personally, I feel that engaging in cyclical limpia rites with water, fire, sweeps, platicas, and spaces limpias should be integrated into our normal self-care routines, especially if we have jobs where we are providing some kind of aid or service to the public. Consequently, the question is not when you need to do a limpia to support the energetic ancestral healing; rather, the question is how often. The stronger we are, the more effective our ancestral healing will be, which will also help to strengthen the bond with our ancestors.

Engaging in regular limpias can be as simple as spraying yourself daily with Florida or rose water, smudging yourself with a bundle of dry herbs, lighting a white fire limpia (see pages 38–39) to cleanse yourself and a physical space, lighting a charcoal tablet and placing resin on it and taking time to journal and release the energy of the day or week, or washing yourself with a limpia soap and saying a prayer for purification while in the shower. Along with making Florida water (see pages 119–22), consider making your own limpia soaps.

Limpia Soaps

Limpia soaps are incredibly easy to make and are also wonderful for clearing toxic energies and repairing any rips, tears, gray fields, or other irregularities in our etheric energy field. The etheric field is the energy field closest to our body that acts as a protective shield around our physical body, and helps us attract more ideal scenarios. You can place a little bit of dry flowers, herbs, or spices inside the soap or on top to bless yourself with their gifts while taking a shower.

Making Limpia Soaps

You will need:

- Soap mold
- Soap glycerin
- Measuring cup
- Soap dye (liquid or powder)
- An essential oil
- Optional: dry plants

You can use any essential oil; just make sure you are aware of the spiritual and magical gifts of the oil. Here are a few recommendations:

ESSENTIAL OILS

ESSENTIAL OIL	QUALITIES
Peppermint	attracting, strengthening, courage, creativity, prosperity, purification
Bay	strengthening our ancestral connections, courage, purification, success, understanding
Neroli	peace, sexual vitality, success, inspiring or seeing truth, courage
Geranium	courage, balance, prosperity, grounding, purification

Directions:

1. Figure out how many cups your soap mold holds by placing water in the mold from a measuring cup, noting the amount of water.
2. Fill the measuring cup with approximately the same amount of glycerin soap. If you are including dry herbs or flowers, remember you will need to leave a little space, rather than filling it to the top.
3. Have soap coloring ready, as well as the oils and optional plants.
4. Melt the glycerin soap base in a low simmer.
5. Once it is melted include approximately half a teaspoon of powdered soap dye or four to six drops of liquid soap dye for one cup of glycerin soap base.
6. Pour the melted glycerin soap into the measuring cup, add about six to eight drops of your essential oils, then pour it into the soap mold, and if you are including dry plants, place a pinch inside the mixture and stir. To avoid spills, make sure that you don't fill it to the top.
7. You can also place your dry plants on top if you are using them.

Monthly Limpias

Any of the limpias below should ideally be done monthly or as often as it is needed. I identify them as monthly because they are typically more time-consuming than spraying ourselves daily with Florida water. We can engage in them more than once a month, and as long as we do them once a month, our energy levels should be strong enough to facilitate impeccable ancestral healing.

Baños

Baños are baths that cleanse the mind, body, and spirit, and they are incredibly powerful in ensuring that our energy levels are revitalized. I highly recommend integrating baños as part of your monthly self-care practice.

For a baño, you will need 2 cups of Epsom salt (to further detoxify the body) and herbs. (If the herbs are dry, use a small palmful, and if they are fresh, use twice the amount.) If you do not have access to a tub, consider purchasing a kid-size pool. All herbs have cleansing properties, and any or all of these herbs are particularly wonderful to provide a deep cleanse and restore our energy levels: rue, rosemary, basil, parsley, mint, chamomile, sage, lavender, and lemongrass. It is very important to take a moment and thank the spirit essence of the herbs for the cleanse and renewal prior to using them. This will strengthen the effectiveness of the limpia.

Cleanse the bathroom or where you have your kid-sized pool by smudging, doing a white fire limpia (see pages 38–39), or by some other way you prefer. For a bath, make sure the water is hot—not scalding, of course, but hot enough to produce a sweat. Place the herbs directly in the tub, or steep herbs in water and then pour this water into the tub. An easy and effective way to steep them and extract their medicinal spiritual constituents is in a coffee or tea maker. Typically, a 12-cup coffee or tea maker will yield 5 to 7 pots of steeped water that will go into the tub. You know you are done with the steeping process when the concentrated tea becomes lighter in color. The preparation for the baño can take approximately 40 to 60 minutes and is well worth the preparation.

While taking your baño connect with the spirit of the water and herbs and thank them for cleansing and renewing you.

While in the baño, I like to engage and invoke my ancestors and guides, thanking them for healing, clearing, and renewing me in any way they see fit. Once I am done with the baño, I engage in a fire limpia with a charcoal tablet and resin, a white fire limpia, or I light a candle and thank the smoke or fire for carrying my prayers.

Scented Velaciones

Our ancestors absolutely love scents as offerings. There are seven-day prayer candles that are scented. Do an internet search if you do not have a *botanica* (a metaphysical store that typically sells curanderismo supplies) in your area to find scented seven-day prayer candles.

If you are going to be or have been included in the ancestral healing, then obtain a picture of yourself. Also get an actual picture of an ancestor or an image that represents the ancestor or lineage you will be clearing, have cleared, or would like to work with to manifest something in your life. These images will be placed underneath your petition.

When writing your petition, start the petition with "God, Company of Heaven, I Am That I Am, please and thank you with and by the Sacred Fires of God's Love and Light for [ensuring, clearing, rescripting, transmuting . . .]" and end with "Thank you. Amen." When I use the term "God," it is free of any monotheistic religious associations; rather, it is the divine principle of the Highest Love. If the term "God" does not resonate with you, use something you feel is divine, that you feel has the power to clear and transmute, whether the prayer be to Krishna, Buddha, Hecate, or any other force or deity. There must be faith in a divine force or principle; this is what fuels the magic in cleansing and renewing a personal situation.

Use any scented candle you like; chances are your ancestor will like it, too. Here are some additional spiritual gifts of common scented candles:

CANDLES

SCENTS	QUALITIES
Vanilla, Jasmine, Lavender	Peace and happiness
Roses, Apple	Purification and love
Berries, Cacao	Success and joy
Cinnamon, Orange	Strengthen connections

Scented candles also maintain the sweetness of the ofrenda during the duration of the velación. Again, do not snuff out your candle. If you are concerned about leaving something lit, consider placing the candle in a water mug and placing the picture(s) and petition underneath the water mug, or do the baño limpia instead.

Engaging in magical limpia rituals, such as velaciónes or limpia sweeps, strengthen our magical mojo, often linked to our ihiyotl animating soul energies, which in turn makes our energetic ancestral healing more effective.

Sweep Limpia (Barrida)

Sweep limpias or barridas are thought to cleanse or eliminate negative or dense vibrations by transferring them into a sacred tool. The sacred tool used for the barrida can be a bundle of herbs, flowers, feathers, or eggs. They purify and prepare the receiver for a renewal, remove dense energies, sweep obstacles out of the way, open up pathways, and invite our ancestors to intervene on our behalf. I highly recommend teaching your loved ones to perform a barrida for you. My mentors taught me that having a barrida facilitated for you is substantially stronger than when we do it for ourselves. When we facilitate barridas for someone we empower it with our tonalli. I have noticed I feel significantly clearer when the barrida on yourself is facilitated for me than when I do it for myself.

To perform a barrida on yourself, place a red yarn on the hand(s) you will be performing the barrida with, covering the center of the palm, where the energy center of the hand is located. If you work a lot with your hands, then I recommend to also focus the barrida as instructed below on the palms of both hands and place the red yarn on both of your hands, rather than just your dominant hand. The red yarn stops the energy from coming back into us if you are doing the barrida on yourself and not having someone facilitate it for you.

This barrida requires a rattle, homemade (pages 119–22) or store-bought Florida water, lemon, tobacco, salt, and a compostable plate. The lemon, tobacco, and salt serve to absorb any toxic energies and revitalize our energetic levels. Tobacco, specifically, is believed to be a powerhouse in breaking hexes and negative repeating patterns. Use organic tobacco. Do an internet search for *mapacho,* which is tobacco that is typically grown organically.

Sweep Limpia with Lemon (Barrida)

Place the uncut lemon in charged water (water that you have stated a prayer over or have obtained from a sacred water source or the church), and leave it in the water overnight, if possible. You will use this lemon to perform a barrida. Before the barrida, please thank the lemon, tobacco, and salt for cleansing you of any unwanted energies and revitalizing you. If you are facilitating the barrida for someone, take a very small amount of Florida water and offer a *soplada* (making sure the water does not go beyond your teeth, blow it out hard as a mist) or spray Florida water from a spray bottle from your head down to the feet, about four to five sopladas or sprays. If you are doing it for yourself, then use the spray bottle. Run a rattle down the body, head down to the feet, a few times to shake the negative energy out.

Then take the lemon from the glass, place it inside both hands, and breathe a prayer into it. Then continue to repeat the prayer out loud while you perform the barrida. Use your dominant hand to sweep the lemon down the body. Start with the lemon at the crown of the head, go down one arm, and then back to the top of the head down the other arm. Go back to the top of the head and move down to one foot, and then back to the top of the head down to the other foot. When moving the lemon down the body, focus on the eyes, ears, lips, hands, belly button, and the bottom of the feet by making small circles with the lemon on these parts of the body or anywhere else you feel may need extra attention. Then, move the lemon around the perimeter of the person's body. End the barrida by being anointed or anointing yourself with your favorite oil or the blessed water by placing it on your forehead, throat, and heart center. The areas of the body I encourage us to focus on are spaces where our soul energies are concentrated. While the teyolía is thought to be concentrated at the center of the chest, I want to ensure that those with breasts feel safe, so I avoid this area and instead make a circular motion above the center of the chest with water or an oil when I am sealing the barrida.

Place tobacco on the plate in the form of a cross, squeeze the lemon that was used in the barrida on the tobacco, pour salt over it, and place it under your bed where your head is at for seven days. After the seventh day, place the contents in a bag and throw it in a trash bin outside of your home, preferably a few miles from where the barrida was performed.

K'AWIIL: LIGHTNING ANCESTRAL SPIRIT AND MEDICINE

Gloria came to me with issues of being stuck in a loop of lack and misfortune. Despite graduating top of her class and obtaining two master's degrees, she was unable to obtain a well-paying job that allowed her to live on her own. Consequently, she still lived at home with her mother and father. She was an attractive lady in her late forties, yet her longest romantic relationship had been seven months. Although she was grateful to have a roof over her head, she admitted to me that her mother was very controlling and domineering and her father was the man who molested her during her childhood. During our plática, I sensed that she had a very strong ancestral curse she was carrying. I performed a lemon barrida for her and gave her some organic tobacco to take home. I instructed her to place the tobacco in the form of the cross and squeeze the lemon over it and cover it with salt, then place it underneath her bed for seven days.

In our next session, she told me that the evening she placed the plate with the salt, tobacco and squeezed the lemon, torrential rain came down in her area. Incredibly loud thunder and bolts of lightning woke her up. She shared with me that she felt that the lightning was moving something out of the way for her. While in the kitchen drinking coffee the next morning, her mother and father were talking about the strength of the lightning. Her mother shared how Gloria's great-grandfather had been struck by lightning and survived. Everyone in the family believed that the lightning turned him from a quiet introvert to a charismatic and enthusiastic older gentleman that suddenly gained a zest for life.

That day before our session, I read an academic article on a Maya lightning and rain deity, K'awiil, and the associations of K'awiil with ancestors, corn, and fertility. I knew this was not a coincidence. I asked

Gloria how she felt about the lightning that evening, and she told me that she loved it. She sensed that it was her great-grandfather clearing obstacles for her. I asked her how she felt about creating an ancestral altar for him. Her eyes lit up and she shared with me that she would love that. I recommend that once the altar was complete, on the next new moon or during the waxing moon, that she also do a baño for herself. Thereafter, I asked her to do a velación at high noon for an ideal job and leave it burning on her ancestral altar. The waxing moon supports growth, wherein the new moon supports the birth of something new. The Sun at high noon would give her petition power. I also recommended that it was critical to invite K'awiil and anything that represented lightning or was made from lightning, such as fulgurite (crystallized sand from lightning), on her ancestral altar. Before I could recommend it, she asked if it was appropriate to include images of K'awiil on the altar. I responded affirmatively. According to her mother, her great-grandfather loved his coffee and pastries. I asked her to make offerings of a sweet-smelling pastry and coffee to him. I also recommended that she invite him to infuse his essence into the fulgurite and other lightning-related items she had obtained.

At her next session, she came in glowing and told me that she had been hired for a midlevel data analyst position earning more than twice her former salary. She told me that the night she began her velación, she had dreams that her great-grandfather came to her and ordered her to leave her parents' house immediately. Although she had not been making much money, she did have a small savings account. She told me that earlier that week she signed a lease agreement and was moving the following week. She also showed me her beautiful fulgurite pendant necklace. She told me that she felt the presence of her great-grandfather through this pendant.

Currently, Gloria still loves her job, her new apartment, has two beautiful ancestral altars, and has been dating a very nice gentleman. Gloria radiates with joy.

Healing Grief from the Death of a Loved One and Facilitating Their Graceful Transition

When I decided that the last book I would write would be on the veneration of ancestors, a wave of new clients came to me to help them heal from the loss of a loved one or as they were nearing their transition into death. While I have worked on these issues before, the number of new clients who requested my help for this was truly uncanny. Those who had lost a loved one carried different levels of sadness and pain, sometimes felt shame for "still" grieving their loved ones, felt they had "inherited" similar illnesses after their loved one's passing, or asked for guidance as to ancient Mesoamerican rites to honor the transitioning of loved ones who were expected to pass or the transition of loved ones who had passed. Reflecting on how these rites have helped my clients to heal and grieve, I felt it was appropriate to make the connections with the rites I have shared in this book and share one additional rite for soul release in this epilogue.

Ritual is a beautiful and incredibly helpful way to process and heal from the grief and pain of the death of a loved one. Thinking about engaging in any ritual to process the pain and grief can be downright frightening and disheartening. This is often because we know we will likely be feeling these heavy emotions in all of their dimensions in these rituals. But trying to hold in the grief, ignoring it on some level, or refusing healthy ways to process the passing can create even more serious emotional, mental, spiritual, and even physical problems in the long run. The pain of losing a loved one may always be felt on some level. The pain is often a reflection of our love for them. With safe spaces of ritualized grieving the heaviness of the loss can become lighter.

When my clients refer to their disbelief in "still" feeling grief for losing a loved one, I ask them what rituals they engaged in to help them process the grief and honor their loved ones. Sometimes, they will have a small altar for them, but it is very rare that they engaged in any ritual aside from a contemporary burial or cremation memorial to honor them. Often this is a beautiful ceremony, but it is not necessarily a space to truly purge in a primal way the grief and pain.

I share with them the wailing and releasing rites of my Central Mesoamerican ancestors. The family publicly cried and wailed for hours and coupled this purging with movement—somber movement, but movement nonetheless—while their community held space for them as they were purging. After hours of purging through crying, wailing, and movement, their community gave them offerings to support them. I also stress that the grieving and veneration rituals continued months and years thereafter.

I typically then inquire if they have anyone they feel comfortable with who would help hold space for them to have a fire ceremony and grieve, cry, wail, scream, and drum, and share special memories of the deceased, how they felt about them, and anything else they want to share to purge the pain. If they do not have access to a fire pit, I recommend a white fire limpia (see pages 38–39). At this ritualized grieving memorial, I encourage them to engage in a primal type of grieving or purging and let the participants know that they will be holding space for this. If they do not have anyone in their lives who will help them hold space or they feel comfortable with, I still encourage them to engage in this ritual and really allow the grief, screaming, wailing to come out. Depending on where they are in their process, I may also recommend creating a pinecone bundle and offering it to the fire as they are purging their grief (see pages 89–91).

I may also recommend having a ritual on the day their loved one passed away, years after their passing, to honor their memory and strengthen their soul energies in the afterlife. If they have a garden and like gardening, I may also recommend to engage in the sacred gardening rites discussed in chapter four, and invite their loved ones to be expressed in their beloved gardens (see pages 114–18).

There are also instances when I feel that my client may have a soul piece of their deceased loved one. It is rather common for a deceased loved one to give us some of their tonalli when they pass, and we may take it, especially if we are having an incredibly difficult time with their passing. When I sense this is the case, I stress gentleness and am very mindful of how to approach this. When we are holding onto the soul piece of a deceased loved one, initially it may indeed help us get through the days, weeks, and months. But the deep heaviness of the loss will generally be very prevalent while we are holding onto their soul piece. After some time, we may also inherit the illnesses, unresolved issues, or unwanted patterns of our deceased loved ones through this soul piece.

I may approach the need for soul release by first discussing the understandings of my ancient Mesoamerican ancestors regarding strengthening the soul energies of our deceased loves ones, so we may strengthen our connection with them, and they can guide, aid, and intervene in our lives more readily. I also let them know that it is common that we may take a soul piece of our deceased loved ones when they may believe that we need it or we are unable to function and are completely devastated by their death. This is an incredibly sensitive area. I never suggest a soul release in instances where I feel they are going to fall apart in any way without this soul piece. Instead, I will begin teaching them alternative practical ways to garner tonalli, such as going outside and connecting with the Sun, especially in the morning and noon, and breathing in the Sun's tonalli. The Sun is one of the most potent sources of tonalli.

When I feel like they are more at peace and in acceptance with the passing and I know they are engaging in energetic self-care limpia practices, especially obtaining tonalli from natural sources and strengthening their tonalli, then I will ask them if they are open to a pinecone barrida to release any soul pieces of their deceased loved ones to ultimately strengthen the soul pieces of the deceased. This allows for a stronger connection with their loved ones, wherein their loved ones can intervene, guide, and aid them, and most importantly the heaviness from the heart can be significantly lifted.

I perform the pinecone barrida exactly as I explained on pages 89–91. After I have facilitated the pinecone barrida on them, I place it in a bag for the client to take home. I ask them that on an evening they feel they are ready, to burn the pinecone in a fire pit or a white fire limpia (see pages 38–39). The white fire limpia will likely need to be done a few times to get the pinecone to burn and become ash as much as possible. While the pinecone is burning, I encourage them to speak to their loved ones, sing a song, play a drum for them, and let their loved ones know how much they are loved. The fire and pinecone both help to carry our ofrendas to our loved ones in the non-ordinary realms. I ask them to bury the ashes or any unburned part of the pinecone. If they do not have a private space where then they can bury the ashes or any unburned part of the pinecone, I encourage them to bury it somewhere beautiful, like one of their favorite spaces in nature. Alternatively, they can lovingly disperse the ashes in a body of moving water.

When a loved one has a terminal illness and they are in the near processes of transition, and my client wants to hold space for their loved one and facilitate a more graceful transition, I share the rites that are highlighted in this book. I generally start with encouraging them to facilitate a plática for their loved ones. Similar to what was discussed in chapter five, I ask them to light a sahumerio with copal. If their loved one is too weak for the smoke or has asthma, I recommend that they use an oil diffuser and along with the essential oils, they replace half of the water with their homemade (see pages 119–22) or store-bought Florida water. Then, I recommend they hold space for their loved ones to release anything weighing heavy in their hearts. One of my clients gave her bedridden brother a water limpia with a sponge bath and a concentrated warm tea of herbs, after the plática. I recommended chamomile, lavender, rue, and lemongrass for this water limpia. I felt these herbs would be strong enough to cleanse her brother, but gentle at the same time.

I may also recommend that a jade stone or another green stone be place at the center of the person's chest, who is about to transition, during the plática or platicas. I only recommend to do so if the person can ensure that the deceased will be buried with the green stone or it will be placed in or near the urn of their ashes. If possible, I also recommend that my client get a lock of hair of their loved ones and place it in a small box or bag that will be next to the green stone when they transition. The lock of hair attracts any soul pieces that are still not with the person, four days after their death. The green stone will carry the deceased's heart soul energy, their teyolía, strengthening this soul energy in their afterlife. The plática helps the person to purge any resentment or anger that may be held, weakening their ihiyotl soul energies. Having someone who loves the person facilitate the strengthening of their soul energies before their transition can be incredibly healing for all parties involved. These rituals are also still believed to strengthen a beautiful, loving, and peaceful connection when our loved ones pass away.

I offer these rituals with deep love and compassion in my heart. I truly hope they help you and your loved ones, if you are guided to use them.

Notes

INTRODUCTION. ANCIENT MESOAMERICAN AND CURANDERISMO ANCESTRAL VENERATION

1. McAnany, *Living with the Ancestors,* 113; O'Neil, "Maya Sculptures of Tikal," 122; Novotny, "The Bones of the Ancestors," 54; Lucero, *Water and Ritual,* 181; Scherer, *Mortuary Landscapes,* 181.
2. Smith, "Excavations at Altar de Sacrificios," 212; Welsh, "An Analysis of Classic Lowland Maya Burials," 15.
3. Houston et al., "Messages From Beyond," 245.
4. Cortés, *Letters from Mexico,* 98.
5. Houston et al., *Temple of the Night Sun,* 14; Schele and Matthews, *The Code of Kings,* 84; Houston et al., "Messages From Beyond," 245. Gillespie, "Body and Soul," 71; Redfield and Rojas, *Chan Kom,* 199.
6. Furst, *Natural History,* 171; Álvarez Esteban, "La entidada animica," 5; Aguilar-Moreno, *Handbook to Life,* 171; Houston and Cummins, "Body, Presence, and Space," 365; Foster, *Handbook to Life,* 187.
7. Maffie, *Aztec Philosophy,* 424; León-Portilla, *Aztec Thought,* 114; Aguilar-Moreno, *Handbook to Life,* 172; Furst, *Natural History,* 180–83; Ortiz de Montellano, *Aztec Medicine,* 45, citing López Austin, *Human Body,* 1:348.
8. Heyden, "From Teotihuacán to Tenochtitlan," 168–84.
9. Bell, *Ritual Theory, Ritual Practice,* 267.
10. Scherer, *Mortuary Landscapes,* 9.
11. López Austin, *Myths of the Opossum,* 15.
12. López Austin, *Myths of the Opossum,* 14.
13. Gillespie, "Inside and Outside," 103–4; Parker Pearson, *The Archaeology of Death,* 141; Gell, *Art and Agency,* 256.
14. Manzanilla, "Houses and Ancestors," 55.

15. Soustelle, *Daily Life of the Aztecs,* 211–13.
16. Kristan-Graham, "Building Memories at Tula," 104.
17. Fash and Fash, "Teotihuacán and the Maya," 447.
18. Schele and Matthews, *The Code of Kings,* 25.
19. Díaz Del Castillo, *Historia verdadera de la conquista,* 244; Levy, *Conquistador,* 153.
20. Houston, et al., *Temple of the Night Sun,* 12, 232; López Austin, *Human Body,* 328; Maffie, *Aztec Philosophy,* 22–23.
21. Durán, *Historia de las indias,* 2:268.
22. Anzaldúa, "Border arte," 113.
23. Medina, "Nepantla Spirituality," 284.

CHAPTER 1. LOCATING THE ANCESTORS YOU WISH TO VENERATE

1. McAnany, *Living with the Ancestors,* 60.
2. Fitzsimmons, "Perspectives on Death and Transformation," 54–56; Freiwald and Billstrand, *Actuncan Archaeological Project,* 75.
3. Gillespie, "Body and Soul," 69; Demarest, *Ancient Maya,* 116; McAnany, "Ancestors and the Classic Maya," 279.
4. Coe and Houston, *The Maya,* 234; 19–20; Weiss-Krejci, "Classic Maya Tomb Re-Entry," 76.
5. Geller, "Maya Mortuary Spaces," 38; Burkhart, "Flowery Heaven," 99; Taube, "Flower Mountain," 88; Ashmore, "Site-Planning Principles," 200.
6. Stuart and Stuart, *Palenque,* 119, 173.
7. Kristan-Graham and Amrhein, "Preface," xx; Headrick, "The Street of the Dead," 81.
8. Scherer, *Mortuary Landscapes,* 216.
9. Scherer, *Mortuary Landscapes,* 229; Geller, "Maya Mortuary Spaces," 38; Burkhart, "Flowery Heaven," 99; Taube, "Flower Mountain," 88.
10. Sahagún, *Florentine Codex,* 6:162; De Landa, *Yucatán before and after,* 57–58; León-Portilla, *Aztec Thought,* 56, 117; Maffie, *Aztec Philosophy,* 203; Foster, *Handbook to Life,* 159; Hopkins and Josserand, "Directions and Partitions," 9.
11. Chase and Chase, "Maya Multiples," 62.
12. Pereira, "Ash, Dirt, and Rock," 451.
13. Houston et al., *Temple of the Night Sun,* 23.
14. Gwyn, *Analysis of Mortuary Patterns,* 23–24.

15. León-Portilla, *Aztec Thought,* 54–55; Foster, *Handbook to Life,* 160; Ashmore, "Site-Planning Principles," 216.

16. Ashmore, "Site-Planning Principles," 216; Wren, Nygard, and Shaw, "Shifting Spatial Nexus," 311–12.

17. McAnany, *Living with the Ancestors,* 52.

18. Olton, "Spaces of Transformation," 274.

19. Olton, "Spaces of Transformation," 272; Scherer, *Mortuary Landscapes,* 199.

20. Scherer, *Mortuary Landscapes,* 207; Stuart, *Order of Days,* 90; Foster, *Handbook to Life,* 161; Brady and Ashmore, "Mountains, Caves, Water," 127.

21. Manzanilla, "The Construction of the Underworld," 100.

22. León-Portilla, *Aztec Thought,* 54–55.

23. Aguilar-Moreno, *Handbook to Life,* 162.

24. Taube, *Legendary Past,* 49.

25. Chávez Balderas, *Los rituales funerarios,* 304; Durán, *Historia de las indias,* 2:291.

26. Smith, *At Home with the Aztecs,* 214.

27. Chávez Balderas, *Los rituales funerarios,* 263.

28. McAnany, *Living with the Ancestors,* 100; Scherer, *Mortuary Landscapes,* 172, 175.

29. Kristan-Graham, "Building Memories at Tula," 106; Mock, "Prelude," 4; Stone and Zender, *Reading Maya Art,* 103.

30. McAnany, *Living with the Ancestors,* 60.

31. Kristan-Graham, "Building Memories at Tula," 104; Manzanilla, "Houses and Ancestors," 50; King, "Remembering One and All," 49.

32. King, "Remembering One and All," 54–55.

33. Manzanilla, "Houses and Ancestors," 49; Sempowski, "Economic and Social Implications," 30.

34. Manzanilla, "Houses and Ancestors," 49; Sempowski, "Economic and Social Implications," 30.

35. Lucero, *Water and Ritual,* 62.

36. Stoll, "Empty Space," 93.

37. Demarest, *Ancient Maya,* 116.

38. Welsh, "An Analysis of Classic Lowland Maya Burials," 186.

39. Barnard, *Living in Ancient Mesoamerica,* 104, 106.

40. Gwyn, *Analysis of Mortuary Patterns,* 101.

41. Gwyn, *Analysis of Mortuary Patterns,* 38; McAnany et al., "Mortuary, Ritual," 131.

42. Barnard, *Living in Ancient Mesoamerica,* 106.

43. Kristan-Graham, "Building Memories at Tula," 102.

44. King, "Remembering One and All," 44–45; Stoll, "Empty Space," 94; Ponce de León and Hepp, "Talking with the Dead," 687.

45. Smith, *At Home with the Aztecs,* 32; Sahagún, *Primeros Memoriales,* 207.

46. Aguilar-Moreno, *Handbook to Life,* 166, 169, 170.

47. McAnany, et al. "Mortuary, Ritual," 130.

48. Durán, *History of the Indies,* 18–20; Sahagún, *Florentine Codex,* 10:190.

49. Quauhtlehuanitzin, *Codex Chimalpahin,* 19–20.

50. Durán, *History of the Indies,* 20–33.

51. Sahagún, *Florentine Codex,* 3:163.

52. Heyden, "From Teotihuacán to Tenochtitlan," 168–69, 179.

53. Kristan-Graham, "Building Memories at Tula," 98, 107.

54. Foster, *Handbook to Life,* 28–29.

55. Zender, "Study of Classic Maya Priesthood," 69; Martin, Berrin, and Miller, *Courtly Art,* 57.

56. Foster, *Handbook to Life,* 204.

57. Aguilar-Moreno, *Handbook to Life,* 304; Foster, *Handbook to Life,* 160; León-Portilla, *Aztec Thought,* 124.

58. Maffie, *Aztec Philosophy,* 270–71; López Austin, *Human Body,* 204–29.

59. Foster, *Handbook to Life,* 178.

60. Ortiz de Montellano, *Aztec Medicine,* 70; Foster, *Handbook to Life,* 178.

61. Sahagún, *Florentine Codex,* 4–5:101n1.

62. León-Portilla, *Aztec Thought,* 125.

63. Durán, *Book of Gods,* 243; Aguilar-Moreno, *Handbook to Life,* 149, 296; León-Portilla, *Aztec Thought,* 126.

64. Furst, *Natural History,* 25–26; Sahagún, *Florentine Codex,* 6:144; León-Portilla, *Aztec Thought,* 127.

65. Milbrath, *Star Gods,* 70; Craine and Reindorp, *Codex Perez,* 49–50; Roys, *Book of Chilam Balam,* 110–111.

66. De Landa, *Yucatán before and after,* 57–58.

67. Taube, "Flower Mountain," 80.

68. Taube, "Flower Mountain," 80–82; Taube, "At Dawn's Edge," 147; Ashmore, "Site-Planning Principles," 201–2; Coe, "Ideology of the Maya Tomb," 235; Miller, "Tikal, Guatemala," 7–8.

69. Maffie, *Aztec Philosophy,* 221, 498; Tedlock, *Time and the Highland Maya,* 178.

70. Stuart, *Order of Days,* 82–83.

71. Aguilar-Moreno, *Handbook to Life,* 302–3; Foster, *Handbook to Life,* 28.

72. Taube, "Gateways to Another World," 82; Foster, *Handbook to Life,* 160.

73. Ortiz de Montellano, *Aztec Medicine,* 70; Foster, *Handbook to Life,* 178.

74. Echeverría García, "Tonalli," 188–90.

75. Sahagún, *Primeros memoriales,* 176.

76. Thompson, *Maya Hieroglyphic Writing,* 251.

77. Aguilar-Moreno, *Handbook to Life,* 165; Sahagún, *Florentine Codex,* 3:41.

78. Taube, *Legendary Past,* 37–39; Boone, *Cycles of Time and Meaning,* 192, 204; León-Portilla, *Aztec Thought,* 108–10.

79. Taube, "Ancient and Contemporary Maya Conceptions," 466; Stuart, *Order of Days,* 90; Foster, *Handbook to Life,* 161; Brady and Ashmore, "Mountains, Caves, Water," 127.

80. León-Portilla et al., *Language of Kings,* 426–33; Scherer, *Mortuary Landscapes,* 47.

81. Brady and Ashmore, "Mountains, Caves, Water," 140.

82. Laughton, *Exploring the Life,* 94, 100; Foster, *Handbook to Life,* 160.

83. Benson, *Birds and Beasts,* 73.

CHAPTER 2. INVOCATIONS THAT WELCOME ANCESTORS INTO OUR LIVES

1. O'Neil, "Maya Sculptures of Tikal," 120.

2. Kristan-Graham, "Building Memories at Tula," 104.

3. Fash and Fash, "Teotihuacán and the Maya," 447.

4. Stone and Zender, *Reading Maya Art,* 109.

5. Houston et al., *Temple of the Night Sun,* 157; Fitzsimmons, *Death and the Classic Maya Kings,* 83; Scherer, "Classic Maya Sarcophagus," 257.

6. Ardren, "Divine Power of Childhood," 135.

7. Stuart and Stuart, *Palenque,* 104.

8. Martin and Grube, *Chronicle of the Maya Kings and Queens,* 195.

9. Houston et al., *Temple of the Night Sun,* 206.

10. Demarest, *Ancient Maya,* 96.

11. McAnany et al. "Mortuary, Ritual," 138; McAnany and Varela, "Re-Creating the Formative Maya," 160; Gwyn, *Analysis of Mortuary Patterns,* 49–50; Scherer, *Mortuary Landscapes,* 62.

12. Źrałka et al., "Burials, Offerings, Flints," 233.

13. Houston et al., *Temple of the Night Sun,* 135, 141.

14. Durán, *Historia de las indias,* I: 453, 352–353; Chávez Balderas, *Los rituales funerarios,* 105.

15. Durán, *History of the Indies,* 291, 293.

16. Chávez Balderas, *Los rituales funerarios,* 68.

17. Durán, *History of the Indies,* 122.

18. Chávez Balderas, *Los rituales funerarios,* 92.

19. Aguilar-Moreno, *Handbook to Life,* 168.

20. Sahagún, *Florentine Codex,* 2:138; Aguilar-Moreno, *Handbook to Life,* 166.

21. Aguilar-Moreno, *Handbook to Life,* 170.

22. Chávez Balderas, *Los rituales funerarios,* 69.

23. Chávez Balderas, *Los rituales funerarios,* 92.

24. Tiesler et al., "A Taphonomic Approach," 376; Gwyn, *Analysis of Mortuary Patterns,* 28.

25. McCafferty and McCafferty, "Powerful Women," 50–53.

26. Mendieta, *Historia eclesiástica indiana,* 179.

27. Chávez Balderas, *Los rituales funerarios,* 10.

28. Aguilar-Moreno, *Handbook to Life,* 167.

29. Durán, *History of the Indies,* 267.

30. Houston et al., *Temple of the Night Sun,* 171; Taube, "Symbolism of Jade," 28–32.

31. Gillespie, "Body and Soul," 71; Las Casas, *Apologetica historia sumaria,* 525; Scherer, *Mortuary Landscapes,* 75–101.

32. Scherer, *Mortuary Landscapes,* 68.

33. Scherer, *Mortuary Landscapes,* 69, 70.

34. Scherer, *Mortuary Landscapes,* 116, 169.

35. O'Neil, "Maya Sculptures of Tikal," 119.

36. O'Neil, "Maya Sculptures of Tikal," 127.

37. Coe, *Excavations in the Great Plaza,* 745.

38. Scherer, *Mortuary Landscapes,* 224.

39. Sahagún, *Florentine Codex,* 3:45; Durán, *History of the Indies,* 285n4; Aguilar-Moreno, *Handbook to Life,* 168.

40. Mendieta, *Historia eclesiástica indiana,* 179; Chávez Balderas, *Los rituales funerarios,* 10.

41. Peterson and Green, *Precolumbian Flora and Fauna,* 76.

42. Headrick, *Teotihuacán Trinity,* 45.

43. Gillespie, "Body and Soul," 69–70.

44. Freidel, Schele, and Parker, *Maya Cosmos,* 189–90.

45. Carmack, *The Quiché Mayas,* 161; McAnany, *Living with the Ancestors,* 100.

46. Lorenzen, "Ancestor Deification," 1.

47. Taube, "Structure 10L-16," 275–76.

48. Taube, "The Turquoise Hearth," 309, 311.

49. Scherer, "Classic Maya Sarcophagus," 257.

50. Novotny, "The Bones of the Ancestors," 57.

51. Scherer, *Mortuary Landscapes,* 136; McAnany, *Living with the Ancestors,* 44.

52. Stuart, *The Order of Days,* 266–67; Taube, "Flower Mountain," 80; Taube, "Symbolism of Jade," 39.

53. Schele and Matthews, *The Code of Kings,* 142.

54. Benson, *Birds and Beasts,* 118; Foster, *Handbook to Life,* 192.

55. Peterson and Green, *Precolumbian Flora and Fauna,* 78.

56. Taylor, "Painted Ladies," 178.

57. Benson, *Birds and Beasts,* 129.

58. Blainey, "Techniques of Luminosity," 182.

59. Martin and Grube. *Chronicle of the Maya Kings and Queens,* 147.

60. Schele and Matthews, *The Code of Kings,* 113.

61. Schele and Matthews, *The Code of Kings,* 225.

62. Houston et al., "Messages From Beyond," 2-3; O'Neil, "Maya Sculptures of Tikal,"120.

63. Stuart and Stuart, *Palenque,* 160.

64. Stuart and Stuart, *Palenque,* 180.

65. Scherer, "Classic Maya Sarcophagus," 249; Schele and Matthews, *The Code of Kings,* 123.

66. Olton, "Spaces of Transformation," 297.

67. Olton, "Spaces of Transformation," 275.

68. Olton, "Spaces of Transformation," 291–92.

69. Olton, "Spaces of Transformation," 293, 296.

70. Olton, "Spaces of Transformation," 299–300.

CHAPTER 3. COLORFUL CEREMONIES
HONORING OUR ANCESTORS

1. Duncan, "Bioarchaeology of Ritual Violence," 362; Hernandez and Palka, "Maya Warfare," 79.

2. Foster, *Handbook to Life,* 166; Healy and Blainey, "Ancient Maya Mosaic Mirrors," 240; Looper, "Women-Men," 72; Taube, "The Iconography of Mirrors," 194–195.

3. Schele and Miller, *The Mirror, the Rabbit, and the Bundle,* 225.

4. Schele and Matthews, *The Code of Kings,* 82; Fitzsimmons, "Perspectives on Death and Transformation," 155.

5. Houston, "Impersonation, Dance," 148–49; McAnany, *Living with the Ancestors,* xxvii.

6. Scherer, *Mortuary Landscapes,* 91.

7. McAnany, *Living with the Ancestors,* xxvii.

8. McAnany, *Living with the Ancestors,* 31, 33.

9. Aguilar-Moreno, *Handbook to Life,* 169.

10. Chávez Balderas, *Los rituales funerarios,* 69.

11. Chávez Balderas, *Los rituales funerarios,* 110.

12. Durán, *History of the Indies,* 149.

13. Durán, *History of the Indies,* 382.

14. Durán, *History of the Indies,* 149–150.

15. Durán, *History of the Indies,* 149–150.

16. Durán, *History of the Indies,* 150–152; Alvarado Tezozómoc, *Crónica Mexicana,* 93; Chávez Balderas, *Los rituales funerarios,* 76, 110–11.

17. Benavente, *Memoriales,* 304–305; Chávez Balderas, *Los rituales funerarios,* 80.

18. Aguilar-Moreno, *Handbook to Life,* 169; Alvarado Tezozómoc, *Crónica Mexicana,* 235; Chávez Balderas, *Los rituales funerarios,* 111.

19. Scherer, *Mortuary Landscapes,* 88.

20. Chase and Chase, "Maya Multiples," 88.

21. Geller, "Parting (with) the Dead," 123; Stone and Zender, *Reading Maya Art,* 55.

22. Scherer, *Mortuary Landscapes,* 97.

23. Houston, Stuart, and Taube, *Memory of Bones,* 60; Geller, "Parting (with) the Dead," 124.

24. Novotny, "The Bones of the Ancestors," 56.

25. Chase and Chase, "Ghosts amid the Ruins," 88; Scherer, *Mortuary Landscapes,* 128–29; Fitzsimmons, *Death and the Classic Maya Kings,* 75; Weiss-Krejci, "Classic Maya Tomb Re-Entry," 74–75, 77–79; Źrałka et al., "Burials, Offerings, Flints," 223, 237.

26. Stuart, "The Fire Enters," 375, 417–18; Taube, "Flower Mountain," 72–73.

27. Scherer, *Mortuary Landscapes,* 128–29, 224.

28. Duncan and Schwarz, "A Postclassic Maya," 142.

29. Chase and Chase, "Ghosts amid the Ruins," 83; Eberl, *Muerte, entierro,* 111–115; Źrałka et al., "Burials, Offerings, Flints," 223.

30. McAnany, *Living with the Ancestors,* xxvi.

31. De Landa, *Yucatán before and after,* 56–58.

32. Geller, "Parting (with) the Dead," 125; Lorenzen, "Ancestor Deification," 3, 7; McAnany, *Living with the Ancestors*, 36.

33. Chávez Balderas, *Los rituales funerarios*, 125.

34. Smith, *At Home with the Aztecs*, 90.

35. Alvarado Tezozómoc, *Crónica Mexicana*, 242–243, 265–266; Chávez Balderas, *Los rituales funerarios*, 219.

36. Chávez Balderas, *Los rituales funerarios*, 117.

37. Chávez Balderas, *Los rituales funerarios*, 112; Durán, *History of the Indies*, 206.

38. Chávez Balderas, *Los rituales funerarios*, 114.

39. Sahagún, *Primeros Memoriales*, 61n28.

40. Taube, "The Turquoise Hearth," 303.

41. Sahagún, *Florentine Codex*, 2:23.

42. Chávez Balderas, *Los rituales funerarios*, 115.

43. Sahagún, *Florentine Codex*, 2:25, 135–36.

CHAPTER 4. REBIRTH, RENEWAL, AND CONTINUATION OF OUR ANCESTORS

1. Stuart, *Order of Days*, 268.

2. Taube, *Major Gods*, 8; Houston and Stuart, "Gods, Glyphs, and Kings," 289–312.

3. Foster, *Handbook to Life*, 203; Álvarez Esteban, "La entidada an, mica," 5; Houston and Cummins, "Body, Presence, and Space," 364; Taube, "Flower Mountain," 72; Stuart, "The Fire Enters," 396.

4. Scherer, "Classic Maya Sarcophagus," 245.

5. Gwyn, *Analysis of Mortuary Patterns*, 3.

6. Foster, *Handbook to Life*, 203.

7. Scherer, "Classic Maya Sarcophagus," 245.

8. Novotny, "The Bones of the Ancestors," 56.

9. Schele and Matthews, *The Code of Kings*, 84 Code; Gillespie, "Body and Soul," 71.

10. Carlsen and Prechtel, "The Flowering of the Dead," 26; Guiteras-Holmes, *Perils of the Soul*, 110; Stross, "Seven Ingredients," 35; Vogt, *Zinacantan*, 372; Warren, *The Symbolism of Subordination*, 57; Watanabe, "From Saints to Shibboleths," 139; Gillespie, "Body and Soul," 72.

11. Earle, *The Metaphor of the Day*, 170; Guiteras-Holmes, *Perils of the Soul*, 143; Vogt, *Zinacantan*, 370; Gillespie, "Body and Soul," 71.

12. Thompson, *Maya Hieroglyphic Writing*, 84–86.

13. Maffie, *Aztec Philosophy,* 180; Ortiz de Montellano, *Aztec Medicine,* 134; Houston, Stuart, and Taube, *Memory of Bones,* 270, 276; Taube, "Symbolism of Jade," 74.

14. Houston et al., *Temple of the Night Sun,* 12; Źrałka et al., "Burials, Offerings, Flints," 243; Freidel, Schele, and Parker, *Maya Cosmos,* 292.

15. Houston et al., *Temple of the Night Sun,* 14.

16. Houston et al., *Temple of the Night Sun,* 232.

17. Foster, *Handbook to Life,* 180–82.

18. Scherer, *Mortuary Landscapes,* 55n29.

19. Zender, "Study of Classic Maya Priesthood," 69; Martin, Berrin, and Miller, *Courtly Art,* 57; Foster, *Handbook to Life,* 204.

20. O'Neil, "Maya Sculptures of Tikal," 120.

21. Martin and Grube, *Chronicle of the Maya Kings and Queens,* 165–166; Kristan-Graham, "Building Memories at Tula," 93.

22. Scherer, "Classic Maya Sarcophagus," 248–49.

23. Stuart and Stuart, *Palenque,* 177–79.

24. Stuart and Stuart, *Palenque,* 173.

25. Scherer, "Classic Maya Sarcophagus," 247.

26. Houston et al., *Temple of the Night Sun,* 157; Fitzsimmons, *Death and the Classic Maya Kings,* 83; Scherer, "Classic Maya Sarcophagus," 257.

27. O'Neil, "Maya Sculptures of Tikal," 120; Schele and Matthews, *The Code of Kings,* 130.

28. Scherer, "Classic Maya Sarcophagus," 254.

29. Fitzsimmons, *Death and the Classic Maya Kings,* 144; Scherer, "Classic Maya Sarcophagus," 252, 256.

30. Scherer, *Mortuary Landscapes,* 62; Stone and Zender, *Reading Maya Art,* 108, fig. 1.

31. Scherer, *Mortuary Landscapes,* 114.

32. Scherer, *Mortuary Landscapes,* 113–15.

33. Furst, *Natural History,* 113; Sahagún, *Florentine Codex,* 6:202, 205–206. Maffie, *Aztec Philosophy,* 22–23, 446.

34. Sahagún, *Florentine Codex,* 6:103–4; Furst, *Natural History,* 84.

35. Furst, *Natural History,* 125–26; Geller, "Parting (with) the Dead," 119.

36. Horn, "Gender and Social Identity," 113.

37. Carrasco, *Religions of Mesoamerica,* 89; López Austin, *Human Body,* 328.

38. López Austin, *Human Body,* 1:361–364; Chávez Balderas, *Los rituales funerarios,* 44.

39. Sahagún, *Florentine Codex,* 3:45.
40. Furst, *Natural History,* 59–60, 75.
41. Chávez Balderas, *Los rituales funerarios,* 68; Benavente, *Memoriales,* 306.
42. Aguilar-Moreno, *Handbook to Life,* 167; Durán, *Historia de las indias,* I:344–345; Chávez Balderas, *Los rituales funerarios,* 69, 83.
43. Chávez Balderas, *Los rituales funerarios,* 45, 122–123; Aguilar-Moreno, *Handbook to Life,* 171.
44. Chávez Balderas, *Los rituales funerarios,* 28–29.
45. Furst, *Natural History,* 25–26; Sahagún, *Florentine Codex,* 6:144; León-Portilla, *Aztec Thought,* 127.
46. León-Portilla, *Aztec Thought,* 125.
47. Aguilar-Moreno, *Handbook to Life,* 165, 302.
48. Thompson, *Maya Hieroglyphic Writing,* 71.
49. Taube, "The Turquoise Hearth," 321.
50. Taube, "The Turquoise Hearth," 302–03.
51. Aguilar-Moreno, *Handbook to Life,* 171.
52. Chávez Balderas, *Los rituales funerarios,* 57.
53. López Austin, *Human Body,* 377; Chávez Balderas, *Los rituales funerarios,* 57–59.
54. León-Portilla, *Aztec Thought,* 126.

CHAPTER 5. WORKING WITH DEIFIED ANCESTRAL SACRED ENERGIES FOR HEALING PURPOSES

1. Taube, "Representaciones del paraíso," 36; Freidel, Schele, and Parker, *Maya Cosmos,* 264; Durán, *History of the Indies,* 282.
2. Stone and Zender, *Reading Maya Art,* 51.
3. O'Neil, "Maya Sculptures of Tikal," 120.
4. Stuart and Stuart, *Palenque,* 169; Schele and Matthews, *The Code of Kings,* 106.
5. Stuart and Stuart, *Palenque,* 226–8.
6. Martin and Grube, *Chronicle of the Maya Kings and Queens,* 12; Coe and Stone, *Maya Glyphs,* 46-48.
7. Boone, *Cycles of Time and Meaning,* 194–95.
8. Sahagún, *Florentine Codex,* 1:1.
9. Sahagún, *Florentine Codex,* 3:1.
10. Durán, *History of the Indies,* 213.
11. Durán, *History of the Indies,* 217–218.

12. Durán, *History of the Indies,* 221.

13. Scherer, *Mortuary Landscapes,* 61.

14. McAnany, *Living with the Ancestors,* 43.

15. Aguilar-Moreno, *Handbook to Life,* 188.

16. Durán, *History of the Indies,* 121.

17. Durán, *History of the Indies,* 243, 290, 380, 481.

18. Barnard, *Living in Ancient Mesoamerica,* 117.

19. Cowgill, "An Update on Teotihuacán," 151; Headrick, *Teotihuacán Trinity,* 32.

20. Marcus, "Rethinking Figurines," 42.

21. Marcus, "Rethinking Figurines," 34.

22. Marcus, "Rethinking Figurines," 41.

23. Marcus, "Rethinking Figurines," 44.

24. Norwood, "Ancestors in Clay," 203.

25. Gillespie, "Body and Soul," 70.

26. Durán, *History of the Indies,* 294–95.

27. Sahagún, *Florentine Codex,* 3:45; Furst, *Natural History,* 59–60, 75.

28. Scherer, *Mortuary Landscapes,* 84.

29. Headrick, "The Street of the Dead," 69.

30. Olivier, "The Sacred Bundles," 207, 212.

31. Scherer, *Mortuary Landscapes,* 89.

32. Olivier, "The Sacred Bundles," 201, 206; Pohl, *Politics of Symbolism,* 26.

33. Scherer, *Mortuary Landscapes,* 83.

34. Taube, "The Turquoise Hearth," 307.

35. McAnany, *Living with the Ancestors,* 61.

36. Scherer, *Mortuary Landscapes,* 84.

37. Scherer, *Mortuary Landscapes,* 87.

38. Olivier, "The Sacred Bundles," 216.

39. Pohl, *Politics of Symbolism,* 87, 95.

40. Stoll, "Empty Space," 95; Pohl, *Politics of Symbolism,* 71; Headrick, "The Street of the Dead," 77.

41. Pohl, *Politics of Symbolism,* 82.

42. Lucero, *Water and Ritual,* 229.

43. Marcos, *Taken from the Lips,* 94–98.

44. León-Portilla, *Aztec Thought,* 89, 93–99.

45. Sahagún, *Florentine Codex,* 1:8–11.

46. Sahagún, *Florentine Codex,* 6:34.

47. Sahagún, *Florentine Codex,* 6:34.

Bibliography

Aguilar-Moreno, Manuel. *Handbook to Life in the Aztec World.* 1st ed. Oxford: Oxford University Press, 2006.

Alvarado Tezozómoc, Fernando de. *Crónica Mexicana: Escrita hacia el año de 1598.* México City: Editorial Leyenda, 1944.

Álvarez Esteban, Manuel. "La entidada anímica wahyis en el Clásico Tardí maya y su relación con el poder ritual." accessed through Academia.edu, 2014–2015.

Anzaldúa, Gloria. "Border arte: Nepantla, el lugar de la frontera." In *La Frontera/ The Border: Art about the Mexico/United States Border Experience,* edited by Patricia Chavez, Madeleine Grynsztejn, and Kathryn Kanjo, 107–14. San Diego: Museum of Contemporary Art, 1993.

Ardren, Traci. "The Divine Power of Childhood in Ancient Mesoamerica." In *(Re)Thinking the Little Ancestor: New Perspectives on the Archaeology of Infancy and Childhood,* edited by Mike Lally and Alison Moore, 133–51. Oxford, England: Hadrian Books, Ltd., 2011.

Ashmore, Wendy. "Site-Planning Principles and Concepts of Directionality among the Ancient Maya." *Latin American Antiquity* 2, no. 3 (September 1991): 199–226.

Barnard, Els. "Living in Ancient Mesoamerica: A Comparative Analysis of Formative Mesoamerican Households." Thesis. University of Leiden, June 2013.

Bell, Catherine. *Ritual Theory, Ritual Practice.* New York: Oxford University Press, 1992.

Benavente, Toribio (Motolinía). *Memoriales o Libro de las Cosas de la Nueva España y de los Naturales de Ella.* Edición de Edmundo O'Gorman. México: IIH, UNAM, 1971.

Benson, Elizabeth P. *Birds and Beasts of Ancient Latin America*. Gainesville: University Press of Florida, 1997.

Blainey, Marc G. "Techniques of Luminosity: Iron-Ore Mirrors and Entheogenic Shamanism among the Ancient Maya." In *Manufactured Light: Mirrors in the Mesoamerican Realm*, edited by Emiliana Gallaga and Marc Blainey, 179–206. Denver: University of Colorado Press, 2019.

Boone, Elizabeth H. *Cycles of Time and Meaning in the Mexican Books of Fate*. Austin: University of Texas Press, 2007.

Brady, James E., and Wendy Ashmore. "Mountains, Caves, Water: Ideational Landscapes of the Ancient Maya." In *Archaeologies of Landscape: Contemporary Perspectives*, edited by Wendy Ashmore and A. Bernard Knapp, 124–145. Malden, Mass.: Blackwell, 1999.

Burkhart, Louise M. "Flowery Heaven: The Aesthetic of Paradise in Nahuatl Devotional Literature." *RES: Anthropology and Aesthetics* 21 (Spring 1992): 88–109.

Carlsen, Robert S., and Martin Prechtel. "The Flowering of the Dead: An Interpretation of Highland Maya Culture." *Man* 26, no. 1 (1991): 23–42.

Carmack, Robert, M. *The Quiché Mayas of the Utatlán*. Norman: University of Oklahoma Press, 1981.

Carrasco, Davíd. *Religions of Mesoamerica*. 2d ed. Long Grove, Ill.: Waveland Press, 2014.

Chase, Diane Z. and Arlen F. Chase. "Ghosts amid the Ruins: Analyzing Relationships between the Living and the Dead among the Ancient Maya at Caracol, Belize." In *Living with the Dead: Mortuary Ritual in Mesoamerica*, edited by James Fitzsimmons and Izumi Shimada, 78–101. Tucson: University of Arizona Press, 2011.

———. "Maya Multiples: Individuals, Entries, and Tombs in Structure A34 of Caracol, Belize." *Latin American Antiquity* 7, no. 1 (1996): 61–79.

Chávez Balderas, Ximena. *Los rituales funerarios en el Templo Mayor de Tenochtitlan*. Colección Premios INAH. Mexico City: Instituto Nacional de Antropología e Historia, 2007, website.

Coe, Michael D. "The Ideology of the Maya Tomb." In *Maya Iconography*, edited by Elizabeth Benson and Gillet Griffen, 222–35. Princeton, N.J.: Princeton University Press, 1988.

Coe, Michael D. and Mark Van Stone. *Reading the Maya Glyphs*. 2d ed. London: Thames & Hudson, 2005.

Coe, Michael D. and Stephen Houston. *The Maya*. New York: Thames & Hudson Inc., 2015.

Coe, William R. *Excavations in the Great Plaza, North Terrace, and North Acropolis of Tikal: Tikal Report #14*. University Monograph 61. Philadelphia: The University Museum University of Pennsylvania, 1990.

Cortés, Hernán. *Hernan Cortes: Letters from Mexico*. Rev. ed. Translated and edited by Anthony Pagden. New Haven, Conn.: Yale University Press, 1986.

Cowgill, George, L. "An Update on Teotihuacán." *Antiquity* 82, no. 318 (2008): 962–75.

Craine, Eugene R. and Reginald C. Reindorp. *The Codex Perez and the Book of Chilam Balam of Maní*. Norman: University of Oklahoma Press, 1979.

De Landa, Diego. *Yucatán before and after the Conquest*. Translated by William Gates. New York: Dover, 1978.

Demarest, Arthur. *Ancient Maya: The Rise and Fall of a Rainforest Civilization*. New York: Cambridge University Press, 2004.

Díaz Del Castillo, Bernal. *Historia verdadera de la conquista de la Nueva España*. México City: Fernández Editores, 1961.

Durán, Diego. *The Book of Gods and Rites and the Ancient Calendar*. Translated by F. Horcasitas and Doris Heyden. Norman: University of Oklahoma Press, 1971.

Duncan, William N. "The Bioarchaeology of Ritual Violence at Zacpetén." In *The Kowoj: Identity, Migration, and Geopolitics in the Late Postclassic Petén, Guatemala,* edited by Prudence M. Rice and Don S. Rice, 340–67. Boulder: University Press of Colorado, 2009.

Duncan, William N. and Kevin R. Schwarz. "A Postclassic Maya Mass Grave from Zacpetén, Guatemala." *Journal of Field Archaeology* 40, no. 2 (2015): 143–65.

Durán, Diego. *Historia de las indias de Nueva España y islas de Tierre Firme*. 2 vols. Edited by Angel Mar a K. Garibay. Mexico City: Editorial Porrúa, 1979.

———. *The History of the Indies of New Spain*. Translated by Doris Heyden. Norman: University of Oklahoma Press, 1994.

Earle, Duncan. "The Metaphor of the Day in Quiche: Notes on the Nature of Everyday Life." In *Symbol and Meaning Beyond the Closed Community: Essays in Mesoamerican Ideas,* edited by Gary Gossen, 155–72. Albany: Institute for Mesoamerican Studies, State University of New York, 1986.

Eberl, Markus. *Muerte, entierro y ascensión: ritos funerarios entre los antiguos mayas*. Mérida: Ediciones de la Universidad Autónoma de Yucatán, 2005.

Echeverría García, Jaime. "Tonalli, naturaleza fría y personalidad temerosa: el susto entre los nahuas del siglo xvi." *Estudios de cultura Náhuatl* 48 (July–December 2014): 177–212.

Fash, Barbara and William L. Fash, "Teotihuacán and the Maya: A Classic Heritage." In *Mesoamerica's Classic Heritage: From Teotihuacán to the Aztecs,* edited by Davíd Carrasco, Lindsay Jones, and Scott Sessions, 269–340. Boulder: University Press of Colorado, 2000.

Fitzsimmons, James L. *Death and the Classic Maya Kings.* Austin: University of Texas Press, 2009.

———. "Perspectives on Death and Transformation in Ancient Maya Society: Human Remains as a Means to an End." In *Living with the Dead: Mortuary Ritual in Mesoamerica,* edited by James L. Fitzsimmons and Izumi Shimada, 53–77. Tucson: University of Arizona Press, 2011.

Foster, Lynn V. *Handbook to Life in the Ancient Mayan World.* Oxford: Oxford University Press, 2002.

Freidel, David, Linda Schele, and Joy Parker. *Maya Cosmos: Three Thousand Years on the Shaman's Path.* New York: William Morrow, 1993.

Freiwald, Carolyn and Billstrand, Nicholas. "Burial 11 in Structure 41 at Actuncan, Belize." In *Actuncan Archaeological Project: Report of the 2013 Field Seasons,* edited by Lisa J. LeCount, 75–95. Belize Institute of Archaeology, May 2014.

Furst, Jill, and Leslie McKeever. *The Natural History of the Soul in Ancient Mexico.* New Haven, Conn.: Yale University Press, 1995.

Gell, Alfred. *Art and Agency: An Anthropological Theory.* Oxford: Clarendon Press, 1998.

Geller, Pamela L. "Maya Mortuary Spaces as Cosmological Metaphors." In *Space and Spatial Analysis in Archaeology,* edited by Elizabeth C. Robertson, Jeffrey D. Seibert, Deepika C. Fernandez, and Marc U. Zender, 37–45. Calgary: University of Calgary Press, 2006.

———. "Parting (with) the Dead: Body Partibility as Evidence of Commoner Ancestor Veneration." *Ancient Mesoamerica* 23, no. 1 (Spring 2012): 115–30.

Gillespie, Susan D. "Body and Soul among the Maya: Keeping the Spirits in Place." In *Special Issue: The Place and Space of Death. Archaeological Papers of the American Anthropological Association* 11, no. 1 (January 2002): 67–78,

———. "Inside and Outside: Residential Burial at Formative Period Chalcatzingo,

Mexico." In *Special Issue: Residential Burial: A Multiregional Exploration. Archaeological Papers of the American Anthropological Association* 20, no. 1 (March 2010): 98–120.

Guiteras-Holmes, Calixta. *Perils of the Soul: The World View of a Tzotzil Indian.* Glencoe, NY: Free Press, 1961.

Gwyn, Christina. *Analysis of Mortuary Patterns and Burial Practices in the Classic Period Burials from the Maya Site of K'axob in Belize.* Thesis. University of Houston, May 2016.

Headrick, Annabeth. "The Street of the Dead...It Really Was: Mortuary Bundles at Teotihuacán." *Ancient Mesoamerica* 10, no. 1 (Spring 1999): 69–85.

———. *The Teotihuacán Trinity. The Sociopolitical Structure of an Ancient Mesoamerican City.* Austin: University of Texas Press, 2007.

Healy, Paul F. and Marc G. Blainey. "Ancient Maya Mosaic Mirrors: Function, Symbolism, and Meaning." *Ancient Mesoamerica* 22, no. 2 (Fall 2011): 229–44.

Hernandez, Christopher L. and Joel W. Palka. "Maya Warfare, Sacred Places, and Divine Protection." In *War and Peace: Conflict and Resolution in Archaeology: Proceedings of the 45th Annual Chacmool Archaeology Conference,* edited by Adam Benfer, 73–85. Chacmool Archaeology Association, University of Calgary, 2017.

Heyden, Doris. "From Teotihuacán to Tenochtitlan: City Planning, Caves, and Streams of Red and Blue Waters." In *Mesoamerica's Classic Heritage: From Teotihuacán to the Aztecs,* edited by Davíd Carrasco, Lindsay Jones, and Scott Sessions, 269–340. Boulder: University Press of Colorado, 2000.

Hopkins, Nicholas A., and J. Kathryn Josserand. "Directions and Partitions in Maya World View." Foundation for Advancement of Mesoamerican Studies (website).

Horn, Rebecca. "Gender and Social Identity: Nahua Naming Patterns in Postconquest Central Mexico." In *Indian Women of Early Mexico,* edited by Susan Schroeder, Stephanie Wood, and Robert Haskett, 105–22. Norman: University of Oklahoma Press, 1997.

Houston, Stephen D. "Impersonation, Dance, and the Problem of Spectacle among the Classic Maya." In *Archaeology of Performance: Theaters of Power, Community, and Politics,* edited by Takeshi Inomata and Lawrence S. Coben, 135–55. Lanham, Md.: AltaMira Press, 2006.

Houston, Stephen D. and David Stuart. "Of Gods, Glyphs, and Kings: Divinity and Rulership among the Classic Maya." *Antiquity* 70, no. 268 (June 1996): 289–312.

Houston, Stephen D. and Tom Cummins. "Body, Presence, and Space." In *Palaces of the Ancient New World,* edited by Susan Toby Evans and Joanne Pillsbury, 359–98. Washington, DC: Dumbarton Oaks, 1998.

Houston, Stephen D., Sarah Newman, Edwin Román, and Thomas Garrison. *Temple of the Night Sun: A Royal Tomb at El Diablo, Guatemala.* San Francisco: Precolumbia Mesoweb Press, 2015.

Houston, Stephen D., Andrew K. Scherer, Héctor Escobedo, Mark Child, and James Fitzsimmons. "Messages From Beyond: Classic Maya Death at Piedras Negras, Guatemala." In *La muerte en el mundo maya,* edited by Andrés Ciudad Ruiz, Mario Humberto Ruz, Ma. Josepha Iglesias Ponce de León, and P. Cagiao, 113–43. Madrid: Sociedad Española de Estudios Mayas, 2003.

Houston, Stephen D., David Stuart, and Karl A. Taube. *The Memory of Bones: Body, Being, and Experience among the Classic Maya.* Austin: University of Texas Press, 2006.

King, Stacie M. "Remembering One and All: Early Postclassic Residential Burial in Coastal Oaxaca, Mexico." In *Special Issue, Residential Burial: A Multigenerational Exploration. Archaeological Papers of the American Anthropological Association* 20, no. 1 (March 2021): 44–58.

Kristan-Graham, Cynthia. "Building Memories at Tula: Sacred Landscapes and Architectural Veneration." In *Memory Traces: Analyzing Sacred Space at Five Mesoamerican Sites,* edited by Cynthia Kristan-Graham and Laura M. Amrhein, 81–130. Boulder: University Press of Colorado, 2015.

Kristan-Graham, Cynthia, and Laura M. Amrhein, "Preface: Memory Traces." In *Memory Traces: Analyzing Sacred Space at Five Mesoamerican Sites,* edited by Cynthia Kristan-Graham and Laura M. Amrhein, xiii–xxx. Boulder: University Press of Colorado, 2015.

Las Casas, Bartolomé de. *Apologetica historia sumaria.* 3rd ed. 2 vols. Mexico City: Universidad Nacional Autonoma de Mexico, 1967.

Laughton, Timothy. *Exploring the Life, Myth, and Art of the Maya.* 1st ed. Buffalo, N.Y.: Rosen, 2010.

León-Portilla, Miguel. *Aztec Thought and Culture: A Study of the Ancient Nahuatl Mind.* Translated by Jack Emory Davis. Norman: University of Oklahoma Press, 1963.

León-Portilla, Miguel, Earl Shorris, Sylvia S. Shorris, Ascensión H. de León-Portilla, and Jorge Klor de Alva. *In the Language of Kings: An Anthology of Mesoamerican Literature, Pre-Columbian to the Present.* London: W. W. Norton, 2001.

Levy, Buddy. *Conquistador: Hernán Cortés, King Montezuma, and the Last Stand of the Aztecs.* New York: Bantam Books, 1994.

Looper, Matthew G. "Women-Men (and Men-Women): Classic Maya Rulers and the Third Gender," In *Ancient Maya Women,* edited by Traci Ardren, 171–202. Walnut Creek, Calif.: AltaMira Press, 2002.

López Austin, Alfredo. *The Human Body and Ideology of the Ancient Nahuas.* 1st ed. 2 vols. Translated by Thelma Ortiz de Montellano and B. R. Ortiz de Montellano. Salt Lake City: University of Utah Press, 1988.

———. *The Myths of the Opossum: Pathways of Mesoamerican Mythology.* Translated by Bernard R. Ortiz de Montellano and Thelma Ortiz de Montellano. Albuquerque: University of New Mexico Press, 1993.

Lorenzen, Karl J. "Ancestor Deification in Ancient Maya Ritual and Religion, Late Postclassic Community Shrines and Family Oratories." *Journal of the Washington Academy of Sciences* 91, no. 4 (Winter 2005): 25–51.

Lucero, Lisa. *Water and Ritual: The Rise and Fall of Classic Maya Rulers.* Austin: University of Texas Press, 2006.

Maffie, James. *Aztec Philosophy: Understanding a World in Motion.* Boulder: University Press of Colorado, 2014.

Manzanilla, Linda. "The Construction of the Underworld in Central Mexico." In *Mesoamerica's Classic Heritage: From Teotihuacán to the Aztecs,* edited by Davíd Carrasco, Lindsay Jones, and Scott Sessions, 87-116. Boulder: University Press of Colorado, 2000.

———. "Houses and Ancestors, Altars and Relics: Mortuary Patterns at Teotihuacán, Central Mexico." In *Proyecto Teotihuacán: elite y gobierno. Excavaciones en Xalla y Teopancazco.* Archaeological Papers of the American Anthropological Association 11, no. 1 (January 2022): 55–65.

Marcos, Sylvia. *Taken from the Lips: Gender and Eros in Mesoamerican Religions.* Leiden, The Netherlands: Brill, 2006.

Marcus, Joyce. "Rethinking Figurines." In *Mesoamerican Figurines: Small-Scale Indices of Large-Scale Social Phenomena,* edited by Cristina T. Halperin, Katherine A. Faust, Rhonda Taube, and Aurore Giguet, 25–50. Gainesville: University Press of Florida, 2009.

Martin, Simon, Kathleen Berrin, and Mary Miller. *Courtly Art of the Ancient Maya.* New York: Thames & Hudson, 2004.

Martin, Simon and Nikolai Grube. *Chronicle of the Maya Kings and Queens:*

Deciphering the Dynasties of the Ancient Maya. 2nd ed. London: Thames & Hudson, 2008.

McAnany, Patricia A. "Ancestors and the Classic Maya Built Environment." In *Function and Meaning in Classic Maya Architecture,* edited by Stephen Houston, 271–98. Washington, D.C.: Dumbarton Oaks, 1998.

———. *Living with the Ancestors: Kinship and Kingship in Ancient Maya Society.* Rev. ed. New York: Cambridge University Press, 2013.

McAnany, Patricia A., Rebecca Storey, and Angela K. Lockard. "Mortuary, Ritual, and Family Politics at Formative and Early Classic K'axob, Belize." *Ancient Mesoamerica* 10, no. 1 (January 1999): 129–46.

McAnany, Patricia A. and Sandra L. López Varela. "Re-Creating the Formative Maya Village of K'axob: Chronology, Ceramic Complexes, and Ancestors in Architectural Context." *Ancient Mesoamerica* 10, no. 1 (1999):147–68.

McCafferty, Sharisse D. and Geoffrey G. McCafferty. "Powerful Women and the Myth of Male Dominance in Aztec Society." In *Archaeological Review from Cambridge* 7, no. 1 (1988): 45–59.

Medina, Lara. "Nepantla Spirituality: An Emancipative Vision for Inclusion." In *Wading Through Many Voices: Toward a Theology of Public Conversation,* edited by Harold J. Recinos, 279–345. Lanham, Md.: Rowman & Littlefield Publishers, Inc., 2011.

Mendieta, Fray Gerónimo de. *Historia eclesiástica indiana.* México: Editorial Salvador Chávez Hayhoe, 1945.

Milbrath, Susan. *Star Gods of the Maya: Astronomy in Art, Folklore, and Calendars.* 1st ed. Austin: University of Texas Press, 1999.

Miller, Mary E. "Tikal, Guatemala: A Rationale for the Placement of the Funerary Pyramids." *Expedition* 27, no. 3 (1985): 6–15.

Mock, Shirley Boteler. "Prelude." In *The Sowing and the Dawning: Termination, Dedication, and Transformation in the Archaeological and Ethnographic Record of Mesoamerica,* edited by Shirley Boteler Mock, 3–19. Albuquerque: University of New Mexico Press, 1998.

Norwood, Lauren W. "Ancestors in Clay: A Case for Portraiture in Lagunillas Style E Figurines." In *Shaft Tombs and Figures in West Mexican Society: A Reassessment,* edited by Christopher S. Beekman and Robert B. Pickering, 195–205. Published in conjunction with the exhibition *West Mexico: Ritual and Identity,* Gilcrease Museum, Tulsa, Okla., June 26 to November 6, 2016.

Novotny, Anna C. "The Bones of the Ancestors as Inalienable Possessions:

A Bioarchaeologial Perspective." *Archaeological Papers of the American Anthropological Association* 23, no. 1 (2014): 54–65.

Olivier, Guilhem. "The Sacred Bundles and the Coronation of the Aztec King in Mexico-Tenochtitlan." In *Sacred Bundles: Ritual Acts of Wrapping and Binding in Mesoamerica,* edited by Julia Guernsey and F. Kent Reilly, III, 199–205. Barnardsville, N.C.: Boundary End Archaeology Research Center, 2006.

Olton, Elizabeth D. "Spaces of Transformation at Temple 1, Tikal, Guatemala." In *Maya Imagery, Architecture, and Activity: Space and Spatial Analysis in Art History,* edited by Maline D. Werness-Rude and Kaylee R. Spencer, 271–305. Albuquerque: University of New Mexico Press, 2015.

O'Neil, Megan E. "Ancient Maya Sculptures of Tikal, Seen and Unseen." *RES: Anthropology and Aesthetics* 55–56 (Spring–Autumn 2009): 119–34.

Ortiz de Montellano, Bernard R. *Aztec Medicine, Health, and Nutrition.* New Brunswick, N.J.: Rutgers University Press, 1990.

Parker Pearson, Mike. *The Archaeology of Death and Burial.* College Station: Texas A&M University Press, 1999.

Pereira, Grégory. "Ash, Dirt, and Rock: Burial Practices at Río Bec." *Ancient Mesoamerica* 24, no. 2 (Fall 2013): 449–68.

Peterson, Jeanette F. and Judith S. Green. *Precolumbian Flora and Fauna: Continuity of Plant and Animal Themes in Mesoamerican Art.* San Diego: Mingei International Museum of World Folk Art, 1990.

Pohl, John M.D. *The Politics of Symbolism in the Mixtec Codices.* Nashville, TN: Vanderbilt University Publications in Anthropology, 1994.

Ponce de León, Ricardo Higelin and Guy David Hepp. "Talking with the Dead from Southern Mexico: Tracing Bioarchaeological Foundations and New Perspectives in Oaxaca." *Journal of Archaeological Science: Reports* 13 (June 2017): 697–702.

Popul Vuh, Quauhtlehuanitzin, Chimalpahin. *Codex Chimalpahin.* Edited and translated by Arthur J. O. Anderson and Susan Schroeder. Norman: University of Oklahoma Press, 1997.

Redfield, Robert and Alfonso Villa Rojas. *Chan Kom: A Maya Village.* Chicago: University of Chicago Press, 1934.

Roys, Ralph L, ed. and trans. *The Book of Chilam Balam of Chumayel.* 2nd ed. Norman: University of Oklahoma Press, 1967.

Sahagún, Bernardino de. *Florentine Codex: General History of the Things of New Spain.* 2nd ed. Translated by Arthur J. O. Anderson and Charles E. Dibble.

12 vols. Santa Fe, N.M.: School of American Research and University of Utah, 2012.

———. *The Primeros Memoriales of Fray Bernardino de Sahagún*. Translated by Thelma D. Sullivan. Edited by H. B. Nicolson, Arthur J. O. Anderson, Charles E. Dibble, Eloise Quiñones Keber, and Wayne Ruwet. Norman: University of Oklahoma Press, 1997.

Schele, Linda and Jeffrey H. Miller. "The Mirror, the Rabbit, and the Bundle: 'Accession' Expressions from the Classic Maya Inscriptions." *Studies in Pre-Columbian Art & Archaeology* 25, Washington, D.C.: Dumbarton Oaks Research Library and Collection, 1983.

Schele, Linda and Peter Matthews. *The Code of Kings: The Language of Seven Sacred Maya Temples and Tombs*. New York: Touchstone, 1998.

Scherer, Andrew K. *Mortuary Landscapes of the Classic Maya: Rituals of Body and Soul*. Austin: University of Texas Press, 2015.

———. "The Classic Maya Sarcophagus: Veneration and Renewal at Palenque and Tonina." *RES: Anthropology and Aesthetics* 61–62 (Spring–Autumn 2012): 242–61.

Sempowski, Martha A. "Economic and Social Implications of Variations in Mortuary Practices at Teotihuacán." In *Art, Ideology, and the City of Teotihuacán,* edited by Janet Catherine Berlo, 27–58. Washington, D.C.: Dumbarton Oaks, 1992.

Smith, A. L. "Excavations at Altar de Sacrificios: Architecture, Settlement, Burials, and Caches." *Papers of the Peabody Museum of American Archaeology and Ethnology* 62, no 2. Cambridge, Mass.: Harvard University, 1972.

Smith, Michael E. *At Home with the Aztecs: An Archaeologist Uncovers Their Daily Life*. London: Routledge Taylor and Francis, 2016.

Soustelle, Jacques. *Daily Life of the Aztecs on the Eve of the Spanish Conquest*. Translated by Patrick O'Brien. Stanford: Stanford University Press, 1961.

Stoll, Marijke. "Empty Space, Active Place: The Sociopolitical Role of Plazas in the Mixteca Alta." In *Mesoamerican Plazas: Arenas of Community and Power,* edited by Kenichiro Tsukamoto and Takeshi Inomata, 193–210. Tucson: University of Arizona Press, 2014.

Stone, Andrea and Marc Zender. *Reading Maya Art: A Hieroglyphic Guide to Ancient Maya Painting and Sculpture*. London: Thames & Hudson, Ltd., 2011.

Stross, Brian. "Seven Ingredients in Mesoamerican Ensoulment: Dedication and

Termination in Tenejapa." In *The Sowing and the Dawning: Termination, Dedication, and Transformation in the Archaeological and Ethnographic Record of Mesoamerica,* edited by Shirley B. Mock, 31–39. Albuquerque: University of New Mexico Press, 1998.

Stuart, David. "The Fire Enters His House: Architecture and Ritual in Classic Maya Texts." In *Function and Meaning in Classic Maya Architecture,* edited by Stephen D. Houston, 373–425. Washington, D.C.: Dumbarton Oaks, 1998.

———. *The Order of Days: Unlocking the Secrets of the Ancient Maya.* New York: Three Rivers, 2011.

Stuart, David and George Stuart. *Palenque: Eternal City of the Maya.* New York: Thames & Hudson, 2008.

Taube, Karl A. "Ancient and Contemporary Maya Conceptions about the Field and Forest." In *The Lowland Maya Area: Three Millennia at the Human-Wildland Interface,* edited by Scott Fedick, Michael Allen, Juan Jiménez-Osornio, and A. Gómez-Pompa, 461–92. Binghamton, N.Y.: Food Products Press/Haworth Press, 2003.

———. "At Dawn's Edge: Tulúm, Santa Rita, and Floral Symbolism in the International Style of Late Postclassic Mesoamerica." In *Astronomers, Scribes, and Priests: Intellectual Interchange between the Northern Maya Lowlands and Highland Mexico in the Late Postclassic Period,* edited by Gabrielle Vail and Christine Hernández, 145–91. Washington, D.C.: Dumbarton Oaks, 2010.

———. "Flower Mountain: Concepts of Life, Beauty, and Paradise among the Classic Maya." *RES: Anthropology and Aesthetics* 45 (Spring 2004): 69–98.

———. "Gateways to Another World: The Symbolism of Supernatural Passageways in the Art and Ritual of Mesoamerica and the American Southwest." In *Painting the Cosmos: Metaphor and Worldview in Images from the Southwest Pueblos and Mexico,* edited by Kelley Hays-Gilpin and Polly Schaafsma, 73–120. Flagstaff: Museum of Northern Arizona Bulletin, 2010.

———. "The Iconography of Mirrors at Teotihuacán." In *Art, Ideology, and the City of Teotihuacán: A Symposium at Dumbarton Oaks, 8th and 9th October 1988,* edited by Janet Catherine Berlo, 169–204. Washington, D.C.: Dumbarton Oaks, 1992.

———. *The Legendary Past: Aztec and Maya Myths.* Austin: University of Texas Press, 1993.

———. "The Major Gods of Ancient Yucatán." In *Studies in Pre-Columbian Art and Archaeology* 32. Washington, D.C.: Dumbarton Oaks, 1992.

———. "Representaciones del paraíso en el arte cerámico del clásico temprano de Escuintla, Guatemala." In *Iconografía y escritura Teotihuacána en la costa sur de Guatemala y Chiapas,* edited by Oswaldo Fernando Chinchilla Mazariegos y Bárbara Arroyo, 33–54. Guatemala: Asociación Tikal Serie Reportes, 2005.

———. "Structure 10L-16 and Its Late Classic Antecedents: Fire and the Evocation of K'inich Yax K'uk' Mo'." In *Understanding Early Classic Copán,* edited by Ellen E. Bell, Marcello A. Canuto and Robert J. Sharer, 265–95. Philadelphia: University of Pennsylvania Museum of Archaeology and Anthropology, 2004.

———. "The Symbolism of Jade in Classic Maya Religion." In *Ancient Mesoamerica* 16, no. 1 (January 2005): 23–50.

———. "The Turquoise Hearth: Fire, Self-Sacrifice, and the Central Mexican Cult of War." In *Mesoamerica's Classic Heritage: From Teotihuacán to the Aztecs,* edited by Davíd Carrasco, Lindsay Jones, and Scott Sessions, 269–340. Boulder: University Press of Colorado, 2000.

Taylor, Dicey. "Painted Ladies: Costumes for Women on Tepeu Ceramics." In *The Maya Vase Book: A Corpus of Rollout Photographs of Maya Vases,* Vol. 3, edited by Barbara Kerr and Justin Kerr, 513–25. New York: Kerr Associates, 1992.

Tedlock, Barbara. *Time and the Highland Maya.* Rev. ed. Albuquerque: University of New Mexico Press, 1992.

Thompson, J. Eric S. *Maya Hieroglyphic Writing: An Introduction.* Norman: University of Oklahoma Press, 1960.

———. *A Commentary on the Dresden Codex.* Philadelphia: American Philosophical Society, 1972.

Tiesler, Vera, Andrea Cucina, T. Kam Manahan, T. Douglas Price, Traci Ardren, and James H. Burton. "A Taphonomic Approach to Late Classic Maya Mortuary Practices at Xuenkal, Yucatán, Mexico." *Journal of Field Archaeology* 35, no. 4 (2010): 365–79.

Vogt, Evon V. *Zinacantan: A Maya Community in the Highlands of Chiapas.* Cambridge, Mass.: Belknap Press of Harvard University Press, 1969.

Warren, Kay B. *The Symbolism of Subordination: Indian Identity in a Guatemalan Town.* Austin: University of Texas Press, 1989.

Watanabe, John M. "From Saints to Shibboleths: Image, Structure, and Identity in Maya Religious Syncretism." *American Ethnologist* 17, no. 1 (February 1990): 131–50.

Weiss-Krejci, Estella. "Classic Maya Tomb Re-Entry. The Maya Corpse: Body Processing from Preclassic to Postclassic Times in the Maya Highlands and Lowlands." In *Jaws of the Underworld: Life, Death, and Rebirth among the Ancient Maya,* edited by Pierre Robert Colas, Geneviève LeFort, and Bodil Liljefors Persson, 71–86, Acta Mesoamericana 16. Markt Schwaben, Germany: Anton Saurwein, 2006.

———. "The Maya Corpse: Body Processing from Preclassic to Postclassic Times in the Maya Highlands and Lowlands." In *Jaws of the Underworld: Life, Death, and Rebirth Among the Ancient Maya,* edited by Pierre R. Colas, Geneviève LeFort, and Bodil Liljefors Persson. Acta Mesoamericana 16:71–86. Markt Schwaben, Germany: Anton Saurwein, 2006.

Welsh, W. B. M. "An Analysis of Classic Lowland Maya Burials," *BAR International Series* 409. Oxford: British Archaeological Reports, 1988.

Wren, Linnea, Travis Nygard, and Justine M. Shaw. "The Shifting Spatial Nexus of an Urban Maya Landscape: A Case Study of Architecture, Sculpture, and Ceramics at Yo'okop." In *Maya Imagery, Architecture, and Activity: Space and Spatial Analysis in Art History,* edited by Maline D. Werness-Rude and Kaylee R. Spencer, 306–43. Albuquerque: University of New Mexico Press, 2015.

Zender, Marc U. "A Study of Classic Maya Priesthood." Thesis. University of Calgary, July 2004.

Źrałka, Jarosław, Wiesław Koszkul, Varinia Matute, Bogumił Pilarski, Bernard Hermes, and Juan Luis Velásquez. "Burials, Offerings, Flints, and the Cult of Ancestors: The Case of Nakum Structure X, Peten, Guatemala." In *Into the Underworld: Landscapes of Creation and Conceptions of the Afterlife in Mesoamerica; Contributions in New World Archaeology* 10 (2016): 207–50.

Index

Numbers in *italics* preceded by *pl.* refer to color insert plate numbers.